THESIXPACK

NZ BOOK
MONTH 2006

THE SIX

WINNING WRITING
FROM NEW ZEALAND
BOOK MONTH

PACK

First published in 2006 by New Zealand Book Month
with Whitireia Publishing

New Zealand Book Month
PO Box 52-016
Kingsland
Auckland 1352

ISBN 13: 978-1-877192-27-2
ISBN 10: 1-877192-27-9

Production management and typesetting by
Sarah Bolland & Clare McIntosh, Whitireia Publishing
Production supervision by Rachel Lawson
Cover design by Neil Pardington, Base Two
Printed by Astra Print, Wellington

NZ BOOK MONTH 2006

18 September – 15 October 2006
www.nzbookmonth.co.nz

We are proud to be a nation of readers. Kiwis are highly literate and many of us wouldn't think about relaxing without a good book, but we want more of those books to have been written by New Zealanders. We want to celebrate and showcase the brilliant writing talent we have, to support new and upcoming writers in our country, to tap into the pride we feel in our literary landscape and show you that, whatever your taste, there's a fantastic New Zealand book for you.

This book is one of the most important things about New Zealand Book Month. Its five stories and collection of poems are the winning entries from the New Zealand Book Month competition. Five of the pieces were chosen by a distinguished panel of judges. The sixth piece was chosen by Kiwis in an online poll. Each of these authors has won $5,000 – and a place in history. We hope that *The Six Pack* will launch the careers of new writers and give established writers a new audience.

CONTENTS

FOREWORD
RT. HON. HELEN CLARK
PRIME MINISTER
MINISTER OF ARTS, CULTURE & HERITAGE

I am very happy to contribute the foreword to this inaugural New Zealand Book Month anthology, *The Six Pack*, which is a celebration of New Zealand books and New Zealand writers.

Our writers make a very valuable contribution to our national life. Our concept of New Zealand, and what it means to be a New Zealander today, is developed through ideas and debate. Without books and writers it is hard to imagine having those conversations.

As Minister of Arts, Culture and Heritage I am very conscious that books, like the arts more generally, enrich our lives. Books can be informative, entertaining and wonderfully escapist. They make this country a more exciting, more colourful and more creative place in which to live. That is why the Labour-led Government works to recognise and encourage New Zealand's writers and creative industries.

I am impressed that the book trade and book lovers all over our country have got behind New Zealand Book Month with such enthusiasm, and our Government is proud to be a supporter too. With *The Six Pack* exposing more readers to the delights of new Kiwi writing and writers, New Zealand Book Month will make a very good start indeed.

INTRODUCTION
JOHN CAMPBELL

Rick Gekoski tells the story of judging the 2005 Man Booker prize. He was one of five judges and each judge favoured a different book. As there were six short-listed books, one of them could immediately be eliminated. But getting from five to one was, as Rick Gekoski tells it, part horse-trading, part manipulation, part *12 Angry Men*.

The eventual winner, John Banville's *The Sea*, is a beautiful novel. At least I think it's beautiful. *The Independent* described its Man Booker triumph as 'certainly the most perverse, and perhaps the most indefensible choice in the 36-year history of the contest', *The Times* called it 'a crashing disappointment' (does anyone use 'crashing' quite like *The Times*?) and *The Village Voice* revelled in outing Banville's 'torrid affair with his thesaurus'.

From which we can conclude what? That literary competitions are about as rational as a meteor shower. Indeed, our own more humble judging for the book you are holding in your hands involved Maggie Barry and me giving the highest possible mark to an entry the three other judges (Sarah-Kate Lynch, Tom Beran and David Kirk) gave the lowest possible mark to, along with the exact vice versa for another entry. Up, down. High, low. Who was right? Bakhtin might have said we all were.

What is important is that you are holding a copy of this book in your hands. Six New Zealand writers now have you as a reader. Welcome. They also have $5,000 each in prize money. Not a fortune by any means, but not a bad pay day in the life of a New Zealand writer. Welcome to that too.

Welcome also to writing of great thematic and stylistic variety. Part of the point of coming of age, which we long since have as a nation of writers, is that our authors are sufficiently confident simply to *write* – that they no longer feel the need to brandish their New Zealandness like a tiki over a dinner jacket. James Joyce wrote of trying to 'forge in the smithy of my soul the uncreated conscience of my race'. And whilst I love the idea that literature can do that, this collection suggests that in New Zealand, in 2006, we don't see ourselves as 'uncreated' but are wrestling instead with the nature of our 'creation'. A different kind of forging is at work.

There is a balance to be reached here. How *New Zealand* should New Zealand writing be? One of the features of modernism is its inclination to be culturally nomadic:

a magpie with big brains. In this respect, I agree with some of the criticism of the *et al* installation at the Venice Biennale. For me, its failing was that it owed too much to a determination to adhere to a fashionably deconstructed frame of cultural reference. Clever? Possibly. Citizen of the world? Certainly. But if you are paying money to have a New Zealand pavilion in Italy, it seems neither outrageous nor provincial to suggest that at some level it should be a *New Zealand pavilion.*

The danger here is what is sometimes, and occasionally condescendingly, referred to as 'regionalism'. Brian Turner suffers this label, and sometimes implicit within it is the suggestion that his poetry is less universal for its geographical orb being so firmly in Central Otago. I disagree. Robert Lowell (Boston and New England), Frank O'Hara (New York) and James Joyce (Dublin) were profoundly regional in their landscapes. But they, like Brian Turner, had much to tell us about life wherever it takes place.

So hoping for a reflection of place, particularly in a collection like this, is not an argument for stories about poi dancing or poems about All Blacks. Nor is it axiomatically a call for nationalism. It is simply to say that as one of the people helping to pick the New Zealand authors in this collection, I hoped our writers would give us something that was both of this country and universal too.

And they did. Although, as I suggested earlier, each of the judges found their appetite for New Zealand writing best satisfied by a slightly different collection of writers. We were judging blind so had no idea at the time who we were reading. For me it was Brian Turner, Briar Grace-Smith (who gets better and better), Philippa Swan ('I'm on the crèche committee and Arabella's got nits') and Kingi McKinnon.

I suspect Tom Beran regarded Kingi McKinnon and Brian Turner as standouts in this respect. For Sarah-Kate Lynch it was Henry Feltham and Briar Grace-Smith. For Maggie Barry it was Briar Grace-Smith, Philippa Swan, Phoebe Wright and Brian Turner. And whilst David Kirk made positive comments about the majority of writers in this book, neither of his two particular favourites made the final six. (See what I mean about competitions?)

You, the reading public, also had a chance to have a say in which voices were presented in this book by voting online at www.nzbookmonth.co.nz. Even there the differences of opinion were obvious in the final tally, although Henry Feltham's story 'Lung' was by far the most popular piece of writing.

So what you have here are the works of six New Zealand writers, along with a laudable determination by the organisers of New Zealand Book Month to get this book, cheaply, to as many New Zealanders as possible.

And perhaps we should really describe this collection as a sampler. Yes, many of our best and most famous writers are missing. But for a literature to grow and evolve and nourish itself, that is as it should be in a collection such as this. There may be writers here you have never read before. Hopefully the discovery will be rewarding. You may wish to continue the judging process yourself. Which of the six do you like best? And why?

If we are very lucky, some of you may even take this collection to your book clubs and stage another version of our judging efforts. Argue the toss. Fight your corner. Consider the advocacy of others. Read, think and talk New Zealand writing and New Zealand writers. That would make this collection a great success.

The organisers deserve thanks for their efforts. So too do all the writers who entered (and each of the judges gave high marks to at least one writer who did not make the final six).

And you? The reader of this New Zealand writing? Good for you! There will be something here for you. Something to enjoy and admire. Something to read and applaud and contentedly recognise as us.

TE MANAWA

BRIAR GRACE-SMITH

When the urge came it was ruthless. A giant horseshoe magnet, unpeeling the woman from her sleeping husband and pulling her through doors and over fences. Making her walk barefoot over dewy backyards and cold roads to a house painted green. The goat never bleated or bared his small soft horns as she rustled past his kennel in silk pyjamas. Instead he'd rise to his feet, tighten his ears and become a small seesaw bucking back and forth, as if he knew her and was expecting food. But she never stopped to pat him or scratch his back. The pull of gravity was too powerful to allow her to even swivel an eye in his direction.

Once at the green house she'd push her face against the window and peer in at the man called Spencer and his children, sleeping. All four bodies rolled into the bed, thin cigarettes, rolling around inside a packet made of sheets and mattress. Every night, the man made whimpering sounds as if he was being forced to play the protagonist in the same horrific nightmare, but the woman never went to him. The children too fretted in their sleep, turning and reaching, waving anemone legs and arms until they connected with a muffled thud to another's hollow belly or chest and stuck on. When she was full from watching, the woman would take the spare key from its hiding place in the meter box and with sticky feet go inside the house to gulp mouthfuls of familiar air. To feel the slices in the benchtop where the knife had missed the bread and press her face against calico-covered cushions. She'd lose her hands in the pile of cloth that spilled from the cane basket, pull out fire-coloured shirts and fill them with every inch of herself. She'd take the conch shell from the shelf, hold it to her ear, and let her left hand dance slowly to the inhale and exhale of the small ocean inside.

Once, she had discovered apricots in the fruit bowl and taken a firm orange bite out of each one. Every night after that there were apricots.

After her night of testing, tasting and trying on, she'd wake in the place where her journey had begun. This was a cream-coloured villa with squares of sky-blue around the windows. A quiet space devoid of goats, children and apricots – all of that she was happy to write off as a dream until she discovered her ankles were caked with dry mud, her feet had grown extra layers of skin to protect them from stones and her face was covered with small hard red itchy lumps. Hives. The woman was allergic to apricots.

And there was her husband, Eru, waiting for her, pretending to watch the early morning weather forecast on SKY television. Fluorescent, waterproof and ready for a day of mending railway lines. Poor Eru, he was a good man. Hard working and honest. He'd loved the woman since they were children, the thought of losing her was incomprehensible so he had shoved it down into his gut but it was starting to bubble and churn. Filling his mouth with a bitter bile. 'Where do you go at night?' he finally choked, turning from the television, which indicated nothing but thunder and rain that day. 'Where do you go that I can't come?' But the woman didn't hear. She was already fast asleep and as Eru draped a blanket gently over her he prayed that she had at least included him in her dreams.

Since she'd had the operation things had changed.

The changes had been gradual at first. Hibiscus-coloured shirts instead of black, a more confident stride, a sing-song way of speaking. 'Don't stress about it, buddy,' Eru's workmate had told him while oiling train tracks and chewing on gum. 'People often make massive changes in their lives after near-death experiences. Your old lady had a heart transplant for chrissakes. Put yourself in her shoes.'

And for a short while he tried to.

But that was before he noticed the secrets that glittered in her eyes like polished gems. So bright was their sparkle that he had to either put on Ray-Bans or not look at her at all. Then she had started speaking Samoan. Sprinkling the odd word like grains of black pepper into her conversations. Not too much but enough to raise the eyebrows of those that knew the woman well. Enough to make Eru worry that she had found someone else. A smooth and handsome man from the islands perhaps. A lawyer or a dancer with a body with skin that clung to his muscles like bronze gladwrap. Maybe even a white-coated doctor who'd injected the woman with his language and given her hives just from looking at him.

Thoughts of this possible new lover distracted Eru so much that while at work that day, he stopped mending railway lines and started to dwell. And while lying on top of a scree-covered cliff, far above the tracks he was supposed to be repairing, he didn't even notice a train carrying cars change course. Veer off the broken lines, and chug through space, over the sea and towards the Chathams, where it came to rest on a reef. The local divers there found themselves prying sparkling new cars from carriages instead of paua from rocks.

Spencer, the man who lived in the green house with the goat outside, knew he had a night visitor. The window next to the bed was often decorated with nose and mouth shapes set into an icing of misty breath. The imprints of other body parts were also left behind, on cushions and cloth. Concerned at first, he'd moved the spare key and called the community constable. He'd had her sprinkle dust and remove prints like miniature spiderwebs from glass and furniture. Pick thick strands of glossy black hair from the couch with tweezers, and gaze at it long and hard with her magnifying glass. The constable's dream was to work in forensics. She'd show 'em.

But when the apricots appeared in a circle on the table one morning, a bite missing from each, Spencer immediately understood that the mystery caller was no stranger. It had to be his Mele. He'd been thinking about Mele when he'd seen the apricots at Pak'nSave that day. 'Mele would've loved those,' he'd whispered, looking at the red, fuzzy and orangely overpriced fruit. He knew he couldn't afford them, so without letting himself think twice he'd loaded ten apricots tenderly into a bag and laid them on top of a six-kilo bag of spuds and an elderly cabbage with yellowing leaves. 'No big deal,' he'd sniffed. 'Apricots are no big deal.' The family would just have to do without something else that week. Washing powder perhaps. Or toothpaste. Or meat. Once home, Spencer had arranged the apricots inside the Italian fruit bowl Mele had been given by her mum last Christmas. After he'd put the kids in bed, he'd sat staring at the bowl sitting flamboyantly, Italian and very still on the table, and let the apricots weave wondrous magic apricot dreams of Mele around him, till he was saturated in the sweet soft hardness of her apricot-flavoured flesh. He was fully involved with gorging himself on this fruit pulp fantasy, when something happened to remind him that his darling Mele was gone. Dead.

His daughter appeared behind him, tapping him on the shoulder, bruising his fruity peel and bringing him back to a house which was now full of the empty spaces Mele used to fill... Mele... Mele... Mele... their bodies had fitted together and made a circle, as bright and big as the full moon. And now, without her form pressing against his, he was a crescent. New and fragile. Without her... without her... without her. 'Can I have a drink of water?' his daughter asked, deftly pulling him back to earth before he floated off once more. 'Only if you don't wet the bed,' he told her, his eyes leaking as his tongue touched the stinging and sour apricot flesh around the pip of his dream. 'Dad,' the daughter said, edging in closer, touching his arm, 'Dad, please come to bed. James keeps kicking. Dad, Dad, we're scared.' But her tiny plea never reached Spencer's ears. His hearing, like the rest of his senses, touch, smell, taste and sight, was in another place.

'She can't be dead,' Spencer had yelled hoarsely that day, falling like a drunk into the arms of an old uncle as the nurses quickly whisked his wife away. And in the darkness of his uncle's suited embrace Spencer thought about what they might be doing to Mele in the room down the hospital hall. It would be a big room, painted white. There would be lots of bright lights overhead. Pearl Jam would be blasting from a stereo in the corner. The surgeon would be wearing a paisley bandana and as he held a sharp silver knife above Mele's breast he would say something he thought was funny like 'Oh I really don't have the heart for this.' Then he would push down hard with the knife, drawing a tidy line of dark red blood. In his mind Spencer has seen the surgeon dip gloved hands inside his wife as if her chest was the engine of the latest Porsche and he its crazed inventor. From her chest he saw the surgeon pull out something glistening and bloody. Her beautiful heart. 'She won't leave me,' Spencer had whispered then, his eyes brimming up at his uncle. 'Mele promised she'd never leave.'

And now Spencer knew for sure that his wife had kept her word. For it had to be Mele who'd been eating the apricots and leaving bits and shapes of her behind.

She wouldn't let him go.

Back in the cream-coloured villa with squares of sky-blue around the windows, things were getting even weirder. The woman had been behaving particularly strangely over the past week, cooking sapasui for dinner and power-walking ten kilometres around sunset. Eru, who had a lisp and hated saying sapasui, hated eating it even more. This whole deal was far too challenging for such a chilled-out guy.

The woman's brother, Tem, was also bamboozled by the latest developments.

He'd called in to see the woman on his way down south, all fired up he was for a couple of weeks pig hunting in the ranges. 'Kia ora, girl!' he'd yelled vibrantly as he burst through the door. 'Talofa,' the woman had responded without a blink. Gregarious as ever, Tem swept her up into his arms and threw her over his back as if she were a freshly slaughtered boar ready to be taken home for the hangi. Normally she laughed when he played like this but this time she was furious. "Ou te le iloa 'oe,' she snapped. 'Alu 'ese mai 'inei!' Her brother wasn't sure what all this meant, but could tell by the tone and the bites, scratches and blows his body was receiving that it probably wasn't very nice. So he'd left, feeling hurt and confused.

Once he was safely aboard the *Aratere*, disguised in a sea foam wig and surrounded by gulls, he'd rung Eru (the woman's husband) on his waterproof cellphone. 'There's something up with your wife, bro. I tell you, there's a makutu on that girl.' After that he'd slunk below deck, to a place overflowing with chunder and the deafening screams of seasick babies. He'd reached into the pouch of his worn leather belt and pulled out his hunting knife. It had originally belonged to his grandfather, a mighty pig hunter himself. The bone handle was warm and yellow with oil from generations of hands. Moving the blade from side to side, he'd watched the light slip up and down its edges and thought about the hearts he'd taken with that knife. When he'd first heard the news that the woman would die unless they found a new heart to replace the old, he'd gone on a hunt to ease his anguish. The dogs had gotten on to the scent of a young boar, and knowing that it couldn't outrun them, the beast had stopped and turned to take them on. Within seconds it'd shredded the tired dogs and ripped Tem's leg open from knee to ankle. So with a bloodcurdling scream he'd slaughtered it and hacked through the beast's ribcage; reaching into the warm and wet chest cavity, he'd removed the heart, still pumping. He'd carried it home carefully and stored it in a chilly bin.

With the bin on his lap and his foot on the accelerator, he'd rushed to the hospital. The woman's own heart was barely twitching by the time he arrived and she was so pale that if it weren't for the black of her hair against the pillow she would've blended perfectly with the janola white of the hospital sheets. 'Beautiful,' she'd sighed when her brother served her the crimson jewel on ice, shiny and pounding with life. With fresh hope, he'd asked the doctor to transplant the heart. 'With this boar's heart inside her she'll never die. She'll carry the spirit of the bush inside and enough courage to conquer worlds.' The doctor had looked at this noble young warrior and laughed and laughed. Once he'd finished chortling he said, 'Transplanting a pig's heart into a human? Even if we were to consider it, which we never would, not after last time anyway, the pig would have to be specially bred for the purpose. I'm talking science here.' Dejected, Tem had gone back home and buried the heart deep in the earth, beneath a young kauri. The tree grew tall and strong and the still-pulsing heart pushed a fresh mound of soil to the surface every day. Even without his body that boar still believed he was invincible.

As the *Aratere* charged through the waves towards the

Sounds, Tem rubbed the scar that ran in a thick and raised cord from his knee to his ankle. The place where the boar's tusk had sliced the muscle as cleanly as an apple and severed the nerves with it. When he got off the ferry, legs as wobbly as a newborn foal, he drove until he reached the outskirts of the thickest bush in the country. Deep inside that bush, amongst a stand of ancient puriri, he set up camp. Living on a diet of fern fronds, pig meat and spring water, Tem vowed to stay there until Matariki, the Maori New Year – long enough for the problem with his sister to either vanish or sort itself out. He couldn't live without her. No one else understood him. No one.

Eru arrived home that day to find that the woman had made a bonfire out of his clothes. When he'd asked her why, she'd replied, the gleam of her many secrets flashing in her eyes, 'Alu e alu. 'Aua ge'i 'e koe sau 'i 'igei!' The husband was so shaken by whatever that meant he'd fled to the pub, something he normally reserved for those occasions when the Hurricanes were playing, or better still the All Blacks, and he needed a big screen to fully appreciate the prowess of the Rugby Gods.

While a small army of friends took turns at pouring his beer, Eru poured out his very sad story. All over the table. 'I reckon she's having an affair.' The army was totally sympathetic (but also a bit pleased, because the night had been fairly boring up till that point) when they heard this news. With their arms locked around him in a scrum of support, they told him there was only one thing to do. 'Kill the bastard. Kill the bastard. Kill the bastard!'

Meanwhile on the other side of town, Spencer (who lived in the green house) and his children lay sleeping again and the woman, as per usual, was picking her way through the night to get to them. Over fences and roads, through backyards covered in dog shit and past the goat who did his normal bucking business as she strolled, loosening the hair from her bun.

Letting the thousands upon thousands of strands of it pour down her back.

Letting herself get taken away by the beat of this strange new heart which now smacked inside her chest like the Tory Channel.

Letting herself give in completely to the pull of the surging tide that was Mele.

Finding no key this time, she marched towards the shed, and without even turning on the light, found the toolbox and pulled from it a razor-sharp chisel. Pushing the rubbish bin up to the bathroom window, she hooked the end of the chisel into the window join and in one swift action prised the whole thing from its hinges as if she were merely opening a tin of baked beans. Leaping from the ledge, she landed on both feet in the sink, sprang up, looked around her, and took in the air. It smelt strangely stale. Not how it used to be back then.

Discarding the clothes she'd been wearing like wrapping paper she walked through the green house sniffing and touching. From the cane basket she pulled out the coloured wrap she once loved so much. The wrap she had bought at the Otara Market when she had visited her sister in South Auckland for Christmas. Feeling the cool wash of its cotton against her skin she remembered the last time she had worn it. It had been the morning she had left this world. Skilled with her fingers, Mele was wearing the wrap in a style she'd created that day, one that skirted and knotted and flounced in various places. She was sitting on the bed, plaiting their youngest child's hair. Spencer had brought her a cup of coffee and was raving about spending ten days on a Buddhist retreat somewhere in Australia. She hadn't been listening to what he was saying because she knew he'd never do it. He just liked playing with the idea of going without food and meditating all day. When it actually came down to it, Spencer was scared of change. But she, Mele, had been lulled by the sound of Spencer's voice, mixed with the smell of coffee and the smooth feel of her child's silky hair in her fingers. Remembering that morning made Mele sigh.

The sound of a great sigh invaded the screaming in Spencer's nightmare and his lids sprang open. Beside him his children slept deeply, one, two and three of them, each darkening their pillows with pools of dribble.

It had to be her, he thought. It had to be Mele.

No longer the tender-toed and silent Goldilocks who came sneaking and stealing in the night, testing and tasting. No longer the Father Christmas who flew down the chimney, or the Tooth Fairy who came collecting milk teeth from under pillows. She was real. He could hear her sighs and small cries as she made new but old discoveries in the house. Photos with curling ears securely tacked to the noticeboard. The drawer of shells she collected from those white sand beaches in Savaii. The tapa that covered the wall in the hallway. The tiny plastic characters from the children's Happy Meals sitting above the sink. Each object no matter how small carried its own string of tiny sensations, memories and emotions. Suddenly the sighs stopped and he heard a muffled . . . mmmmm . . . mmmmm.

The end-of-season apricots.

She was gorging herself on them.

And after all these months of waiting, Spencer found himself scared of what he was actually waiting for. What if she, his beautiful Mele, had turned into a Medusa; an evil-faced woman with hair made of snakes? What if she had no head? But then, how was she managing to sigh and eat apricots? The whole thing was filled with endless and terrifying possibilities. Rolling the kids back over to their own side of the bed, Spencer almost wished that they'd wake and say, 'It'll be all right, Daddy, it's only Mum.' But they didn't.

She had placed a hundred tiny pink candles (left over from when their daughter was born) in corners and recesses around the room. They sent small bright circles of light over the floor and walls, over Spencer's striped pyjamas, over all of her colours. She was in the middle of devouring the very last apricot in the bowl when at last he found the courage to speak her name. 'Mele.' Hearing this, she stopped and spat the fruit from her mouth, letting it slide down her chin. 'Mele.' But she didn't turn around. So he said 'Mele' again only louder this time because for once he had a reason to say it. The owner of those four letters strung together to make a name, his Mele, was standing in front of him. Only she looked different now, well what he could see of her did. Her body was like a young birch tree. There were no curves or folds to it. It held no surprises. It was a line, simple, straight and tall. 'Didn't they feed you in heaven, darling?' he laughed. But the laugh fell flat on the floor between them. For minutes there was nothing but the sound of their breathing and the flickering of one hundred tiny flames. When she finally spoke, her voice was so small and thin, the moment so magic and strange, that Spencer believed that if he moved too suddenly or made a noise it might all turn into nothing. So he stayed still and shut up.

'Spencer, 'ua leva ona 'ou fia sau e va'ai 'outou. I have something I need to say,' she began. 'When I left you I was pulled upwards. Into the belly of a dark grey sky. Up there I flew with the thunder. I danced with the lightning. I let the rain wash me clean. Then I warmed myself like a fat lizard under a bright white sun. The wind blew up from the south and twisted itself into a blanket around my spirit self, pulling me down into a teal sea. I swum like a seal amongst the weed and the shadows until I found her. My guardian, the shark. I held on to her and she took me on a journey through the Pacific. She told me it was time to farewell my many relations. My grandmothers, my sisters and brothers, my cousins. They all knew I was there. They waved out to me as they cast their nets. They sung me goodbye as they watched their children play. They called to me as they rode white horses along black shores. Then from far across the sea I heard your voice call out. You were pulling me back. So I started to walk. I strode like Jesus over the water, then over land, following the drumbeat of my old heart into the suburbs of this city. When I found my heart I walked some more. I walked till my feet were cracked. I walked till my bones ached. I walked until my throat was dry. And I didn't stop walking till I found you. And I was made so sad with what I saw. This is a place of the past. Children cannot be children here. There's nothing to feed them on but echoes. Let this family live again. Let me see where the shark wants to take me. When you're an old frail man call to me again and I'll come find you.'

His wife it seemed was as strong-willed in death as she had been in life, and although he didn't want to, Spencer started to understand that what is gone is not lost, that journeys can only ever go forward and never back. The spell that held him to her was broken and he was able to let Mele, his wife, his love, the mother of his children, go on. With her back still to him, Mele raised her arms skyward and called to the heavens to take her. There was a roll of thunder, a crack of lightning and she was gone.

And finally, the woman (from the cream-coloured house) who had been waiting in the world of waking dreams for what seemed like forever returned to her body with a thump. The first thing she felt was an unpleasant sting. Raising a finger to her face she could feel the hard swelling of hives. Taking in her surroundings, she saw she was in a house that wasn't hers, wearing a wrap whose colours were far too bold for her liking. When she finally managed to turn a full 360 degrees she saw a man in pyjamas standing a short distance away from her. He was doing his very best not to look at her face. But the woman wasn't scared or angry or even confused, because even though this man was a stranger to her, she understood him completely. She knew without doubt he had a raised mole on the back of his neck (on the right-hand side). That next to the mole was a tiny scar. This was where his brother had hit him with a dart when they were kids. She knew that the man talked in his sleep. That he complained non-stop when he was crook but made up for it, because when someone else was feeling ill there was nothing he wouldn't do for them.

A part of the woman loved this man she didn't even know.

'Sometimes you have to hold on so you can actually let go,' she said out of nowhere. Then taking a step forward the woman took hold of Spencer's tired arms and placed them around her tree-like waist. While he shuddered with the pain of having just said goodbye the woman held him in a tight and viny embrace. As he lay on the couch she stroked his hair and listened to him speak of the memories he had with his Mele. These poured from his mouth like the Huka Falls and eventually, when the torrent of them had turned into a stream, which had turned into a trickle ... and the candles were nothing but wicks floating in tiny wet pools, the woman told Spencer, goodbye.

Back in the green house Eru had started packing clothes. The idea of murdering his wife's supposed lover, of cutting him up and feeding his arms, legs and private parts into his mate's wood shredder had lifted his spirits for a short time but had worn off around the same time as the buzz of the beer and talk. Eru was not a violent man. But that didn't mean he wasn't passionate and the thought of his wife with someone else made him want to do something extreme. If not to others, to himself. Eru thought of turning himself inside out and facing his intestines, liver and kidneys to the world, of wearing his brains on his skull like a squishy grey hat. He imagined the local dogs ravaging his out-facing spleen and magpies pecking at his out-facing oesophagus. He saw a small child taking away his perfect pink lungs for a science project. He could see himself sitting in a wobbly wet inside-out heap being interviewed by John Campbell for his television show.

'This is an absolutely impressive feat, Eru,' John would enthuse. 'Firstly, tell us all, is this the first time you've actually turned yourself inside out, and then I personally want to know exactly why you did it.'

'Um, as a little fulla I was very shy so turning myself inside out seemed a good way of getting attention.'

'But it's so incredibly dangerous, Eru, I mean you're

like a slab of ugly raw meat. Aren't you afraid of being accidentally picked up by some council rubbish truck and taken to the tip ... I mean ... does it hurt?'

'Yeah, John. It hurts a lot and I understand that I'm putting my life in danger, but for me, life really isn't worth living any more.'

'Oh come on, Eru. You're a handsome and intelligent young man. You have everything going for you. How can you say that?'

'Because the love of my life has left me for another man.'

The inside-out Eru would squirt and bleed and spit and wobble this information at John Campbell, knowing full well that somewhere in Hataitai the woman and her new lover were sitting on a leather couch watching the show. The act of Eru turning inside out would move the woman so much that she'd scream, 'What the hell have I done, letting that fulla go? Nobody else could ever love me that much.' Then turning to face her lover she would hiss her closing remark, 'Especially not you, you arsehole.' And with that the woman would come running back home.

The packing of clothes, the binding of suitcases and the intense fantasising had made Eru very hungry. He was just shovelling his third plateful of scrambled eggs into his mouth when the kitchen door creaked open.

He tried to ignore the woman when she stood beside him and stared directly his way as if to say, 'Look into my eyes, no secrets now.' He attempted a small bit of resistance when she pulled his eggy fork from his hand and threw it in the sink. He murmured something that sounded slightly like 'I'm leaving you' when the woman's hand lightly brushed the three-day stubble on his face. But when she wrapped those long arms of hers around him and he felt the beating of her heart, like children's fingers, tap tap tapping against the hollow of his back, Eru just couldn't stop his own heart from answering the call.

So these two hearts, one first-hand, one second, kept drumming and tapping and gonging and playing with half beats and full until they found their old rhythm. She was back.

THE LIFE COACH

PHILIPPA SWAN

It was on the same day Becky's husband announced he was moving into their Skyline garage that Becky decided to become a life coach.

'A life coach?' said Erica, on a late night call from London. 'Aren't you being hasty? Maybe you should take more time.'

'Too late, I've already joined an online course.'

'Really?'

'Yeah, it's amazing – I can train from home and it only takes six weeks to become fully qualified.'

'Who with?'

'Well, that's the funny thing – there's no regulatory body, which everyone at ReInventYourself! thinks is really terrible.'

'Reinvent yourself?'

'Yeah, it's affiliated to some big university in Illinois. I'm doing an Advanced Diploma in Life Skills and I'm going to specialise in work/life balance for working mothers. The important thing is that I'll have a good qualification, but you know what? Some people call themselves a life coach without any training! Daishen says that can be really dangerous. He's my personal online coach. Honestly, Erica, he's so supportive.'

'Did you tell him about Bevan moving into the sleep-out?'

'Yes, he likes my positivity. Look, I can tell what you're thinking but it's something I really want to do, so please, show some enthusiasm. Anyway, I only rang because I need a practice client and when I told Daishen you're almost forty and living alone in Hounslow he said you were perfect.'

'Thanks.'

'He mentioned life directional issues and possible anxiety attacks.'

'Not yet but there's still hope.'

'I'll be ringing every Sunday morning, your time, for the next six weeks and I'll also email some stuff. Is that okay?'

'I guess so.'

'Thanks Erica, you're wonderful. Oh, and you'll need to do a couple of assignments.'

Hi Erica!
Below is a copy of your Client Profile. Let me know what you think.

Client A is 37 and lives alone in a semi in Hounslow. She works in middle-management for the National Health Service making efficiency gains by getting old people to die quickly while playing balloon tennis (cheaper than buying dialysis machines).

Client A's interests include rambling in the Pennines and keeping honeybees (she is secretary of a local bee club). She has no interest in cooking or decorating her house.

Client A was raised in a medium-sized New Zealand city best known as a transportation node. Growing up, she was an avid reader and dreamed of becoming a writer.

Client A has had a series of unsuitable boyfriends which may be linked to her father leaving the family when she was 16 to live with a rates clerk.

'What's with the transportation node?'

'Oh that. I didn't want Daishen getting the wrong idea about Palmy, you know, *Lord of the Rings* stuff. Americans all seem to think we live on mountainsides.'

'And what do you mean, I have no interests?'

'I didn't say that, I said you're not interested in cooking or making your house look nice.'

'Should I be? Don't judge me by your values, Becky. There's some pop psychology word for it – transference? Anyway, it's very unprofessional. And something else – I'm no longer a beekeeper, they buggered off last Friday.'

'Really?'

'Yep. Right now, somewhere in London there are eight hundred of my honeybees buzzing about – if only I knew which bloody area code.'

'Why did they leave?'

'Hard to say, sometimes it just happens, only it's a bit embarrassing and I don't want the bee club to know.'

'I know, I'm on the crèche committee and Arabella's got nits.'

'Speaking of which, how are the darlings?'

'They seem okay but James needs remedial reading.'

'That's not so bad.'

'Yes it is, he started watching Baby Einstein videos at two months.'

'Which only proves they don't work. Ask for your money back.'

'Funnily enough, that's what Bevan said. He's always giving me a hard time about the flash cards and omega-3. The problem is, Bevan's greatest aspiration for his son is for him to become a computer programmer. If that's all I thought he might be I wouldn't bother with the salmon. It costs a fortune.'

'Salmon?'

'Oil-rich fish is full of omega-3 which makes the brain wires take random leaps, sort of like welding sparks.'

'And that's a good thing?'

'Einstein ate cod.'

'At least cod isn't pumped with orange dye. I bet your kids glow in the dark – and it's not from the multivitamins.'

'Don't be silly, they have a perfectly balanced diet. They don't need multivitamins.'

Erica lets herself out the back door and goes over to her hive. It's unusual for a whole colony to buzz off together – something must have bothered them. She might as well give the hive a clean, they won't be coming back. Using her hive tool, she levers off the lid and begins removing the frames, her thoughts turning to Becky.

A life coach! Becky – with her history of hare-brained

ideas and half-started degrees, advising others how to improve their lives. Of course it's all Bevan's fault – Becky has a habit of adopting random ideas when stressed. During their final year exams Becky had converted to macrobiotics after reading about brain food, expecting the rest of the flat (including a second row lock) to eat pistachio rissoles. And later, when dumped by a stockbroker boyfriend she took up with Volunteer Service Abroad (thankfully this phase took place in Cambodia), during which time she wrote letters home on the evils of consumerism. But you could always rely on Becky to come out the other side, mildly embarrassed but unrepentant, weathering the jibes with typical good nature. Erica would just have to wait for this life coach thing to pass.

'I want to start by asking what you most like about Erica?'

'Becky, please, don't ask such crap.'

'I have to, I've got to email a summary to Daishen tomorrow. Answer the question.'

'Only if you promise not to use the third person. Well, I like the way I'm a beekeeper.'

'Why?'

'Not many people like bees – it's pretty selfless, looking after something that stings. I know dogs can bite but not usually when you're trying to feed them.'

'I like the word "selfless", Erica.'

'Really?'

'Yeah. It's something we mothers feel, especially when breastfeeding a biting baby. I'm wondering if there's a connection between your bees and...'

'Becky! I'll hang up if you say my bees are substitute children.'

'But I'm supposed to look for linkages.'
'Not with me.'

Becky bounces through the school gates on her Nike Air trainers, her newly washed hair swinging from side to side like a curtain. She feels great! This morning she has cleaned out the pantry, made a chicken pie and spent an hour with Arabella on shape and number recognition. After parent help in James' classroom she will go to the gym. She watches herself. She is her own movie. She is a woman in control.

'Do you ever feel like you're in the movies?' she asks Erica.

'Yeah, sometimes, like passing Marble Arch in a double-decker bus – I'm sure I've seen that in a film. And you?'

'Oh, not really.' Becky gives a small laugh. 'They don't shoot many movies at the entrance to Central Normal School. So what are you doing today?'

'Dunno. There's a good exhibition at the Tate – how about you?'

'I have to clean Felicity's cage – the class rat. She hates me.'

'And otherwise, are you coping?'

'I think so. I'm keeping really busy.'

'You still haven't told me why Bevan moved into the sleep-out.'

'He found someone from New Mexico on the internet. Apparently she likes drinking red wine by the fire and beach-walking in the rain.'

'There are no beaches in New Mexico.'

'Really?'

'No, anyway, I thought everyone liked drinking red wine by the fire. I know you do.'

'We don't have a fireplace.'

'Doesn't matter. Everybody has an idealised vision of themselves but it doesn't mean it's true.'

'But it can be! Daishen says we all have the power to reinvent ourselves. Did you ever think that life is simply a matter of choosing who you want to be and then finding the right path?'

'Uh, no. So how does that explain Bevan taking the path to the garage?'

'Don't know, but maybe it's for the best – opening up my new future as a life coach.'

'And you didn't notice him on the internet?'

'No. I was at scrapbooking night classes.'

'What?'

'Scrapbooking – don't pretend you don't know.'

'Honestly, Becky, I've never heard of it. I'm not sure scrapbooking has come to Hounslow.'

'It's about putting photos and stuff together. If you must know, it's the decorative presentation of family life.'

Erica gave a shout of laughter. 'So while you're documenting your domestic bliss, Bevan is having cybersex with Miss Pina Colada.'

'Who?'

'If you like pina col-ada, taking walks in the rain . . .'

Erica continues to worry about Becky but who can she call? Obviously not Bevan, and certainly not Becky's mother. When it comes to wallpapering over the cracks in life, Claudia Lockyard has the skills of a paperhanger, living a life of style and distinction (or as much as possible when married to an engineer in a transportation node). Erica is sure Claudia Lockyard doesn't know about Bevan in the Skyline – she's only just forgiven him for being called Bevan.

Neither does Erica want to call Becky's friends. Becky has managed to turn motherhood into an art form and, like her mother, doesn't like the cracks to show. Erica had become alarmed during a visit several years ago, having been appointed Arabella's godmother. She had been dragged along to a mothers' morning, promising not to mention James' night nappy or Arabella's dummy, but had still managed to blunder.

'You shouldn't have mentioned the baby's ears,' Becky said later, angrily scraping brown edges off the toast (carcinogenic).

'But did you see him from the back? His ears were like wing mirrors.' Erica was spooning a disgusting mixture of pumpkin and Becky's breast milk into Arabella. Breast milk!

'You don't say things like that, it's a support group.'

'So why pretend to be happy? All that smiling is unnatural.'

'Not as unnatural as getting old people to die quickly.'

'I'll ignore that, but tell me, aren't you guys ever honest with each other?'

'Sometimes. Remember Diane with the cracked nipples?'

'And the fat kid?'

'A good eater, that's right. Kayla. Turns out she eats nothing but chicken-flavoured crackers. Diane's only just confessed. It's hard when you think every other kid eats broccoli.'

Erica never bothers to defend her job to Becky who has decided it couldn't possibly be interesting working for the NHS. But Erica enjoys her job – it's not about getting old people to die quickly, rather to enhance their quality of life. Inactivity increases their risk of diabetes, thrombosis and falls, and Erica's team is looking at ways to encourage fitness. This is a difficult task since there are many barriers to exercise, most notably that oldies prefer to watch *Emmerdale Farm*.

> Erica
> It's time to think about your support team! You need to surround yourself with positive people who can assist your journey to a more successful life. Assess those around you - can they be of help? Remember! You may need to widen your social network. Look for role models - how have they achieved their success?

Becky doesn't think she'll bother with the Pilates classes, it's so boring. Today she feels great, like she can cope with anything – which is obviously more than Pilates. She puts Arabella into crèche and goes to a CardioSpin class followed by StepEasy followed by an argument with the crèche manager who complains about Arabella's conjunctivitis.

Afterwards, she decides to skip mothers' group at Maxine's house. Becky can't stand Maxine, a part-time lawyer who has recently produced her third child just to show the group how easy it is. According to Maxine, having her children by caesarian section has not only spared her clients inconvenience but allowed her to remain vaginally intact! Despite being on the board of several publicly listed companies, Maxine places great importance on these mothers' mornings (as she is keen on reminding them), which has the effect of briefly elevating their slovenly housebound lives. For this they will forgive Maxine her bottle-fed babies.

Becky tries very hard not to think about Maxine who

is obviously the perfect role model. Maxine is everything a woman should aspire to. She is the epitome of personal fulfilment and professional success. She is also a cow.

'Erica? I've spoken to Daishen and he thinks we should spend less time on bees and more time on boyfriends.'

'Well I'm more concerned with my bees – a swarm was sighted in Hyde Park yesterday but they buzzed off before the swarm collector arrived!'

'Daishen thinks your bees are a defence mechanism.'

'And do you know what I think of Daishen?'

'I know, he warned me about hostility. Now tell me, what do you think the men in Erica's life most value about her?'

'No answer.'

'Oh. Well, as a single person living by yourself, do you ever have a sense of irrelevance?'

'Becky, if this is your idea of being a life coach, it sucks.'

Erica
I'm really sorry about last night. I know I'll make a hopeless life coach and I'm going to ask Daishen if I can get some of the money back. Unfortunately I don't like my chances, and I still haven't told Bevan about the course. Anyway, I'm really sorry to have bothered you and thanks for your patience. Take care.
Love B xxx

Erica pulls out a photo album and turns to her seventh form class photograph. Tall sporty Becky in the back row, blonde hair pulled back in a ponytail. She looks for herself wedged among the others, dark-eyed and intense. What happened to her classmates? Given Palmerston North's location as a transportation node, an over-representation in the services and light industry was always to be expected and many had gone on to become involved in sliding doors and packaging.

Erica had spent a varsity holiday working in a flimsily clad warehouse on Tremain Avenue, stacking cardboard cartons. She had been fascinated by the office girl pushing back her cuticles with a biro and laughing with the boys in blue overalls who leant against her aluminium door frame. Erica would listen to her tip-tapping across the vast concrete floor in her high heels in search of the manager, a clutch of invoices to be signed. Erica was going to be a writer and everything was new material. She spent her evenings scrawling in a journal... *tip-tapping across the vast concrete floor...*

> Becky
> Don't give up now! I think you'll make a great life-coach
> - you've always been a good listener and you put so much
> enthusiasm into everything. Please. I'll be expecting your call
> on Sunday morning.
> xxx

Disaster! Becky finds herself in the supermarket queue with the head of the school fundraising committee. This year it's to be a Kitchens & Coffee Ramble. It should have been the perfect opportunity to offer assistance – only there's a sachet of Bushells Smooth Blend lying in her trolley! She wants to die. *Remember, Becky, write down three nice things that have happened today.*

'Daishen thinks we should start setting life goals. Ideally speaking, Erica, what would your typical day be in five years?'

'Just like this. Sitting on the back doorstep with a mug of coffee and the Sunday papers.'

'Really? You want your life to be the same?'

'Sort of. Some things might be different but basically the same. Why do I have to want change? I'm quite content with my life, and that's quite radical in a world geared to selling stuff to make me happier. Maybe the most elusive thing in this world is contentment.'

'Contentment?' Becky sounds worried. 'We haven't covered that yet.'

'I doubt it's in the syllabus.'

'But what about your job? You must want a career change.'

'Not now. I know you find it hard to believe but I get a lot of satisfaction from my job. And in five years' time, who knows? But I'm happy to leave that to providence.'

'I'm not sure providence is in the syllabus either. But Erica, what am I supposed to do? You're Client A, you can't be content – I'll put you down as change averse. Let's try again. It's a typical Monday in five years' time and you're really excited about your day. Tell me about it.'

'I'm off to work.'

'It's dark and raining and the Tube is full. Try something else.'

'I'm working from home?'

'Good, but not in your horrible semi.'

'Why not?'

'I'm sorry Erica, but I won't let your fantasy be set in Hounslow. Now, let's focus on what you're doing.'

'Selling Amway?'

'Writing a novel!'

'Becky, I can't afford to write – I need to pay rent.'

'Self-limiting beliefs! Now here's your homework: write

down all the negative thoughts blocking the path to your new ideal self and then write a positive statement beside each.'

A couple of minutes later the phone rings. It's Becky again. 'Erica! I've just remembered!'

'What?'

'D'you remember *66 Charing Cross Road*?'

'Wasn't it 84?'

'Whatever, with Anthony Hopkins and Glenda Jackson. That's you! Remember the typewriter and all her books? I know it's you!'

'I think it was Anne Bancroft.'

'Yeah, well I think you should watch it. And take notes.'

Erica drags her beanbag over to the television, thinking about Becky. The truth is, Becky has never forgiven Erica for taking the high moral ground, for choosing to remain single rather than compromise herself by marrying someone barely satisfactory. Making singledom a choice (for surely she could have married had only she applied herself!) was to thumb her nose at all Becky had achieved. Becky's response was mild condescension – nothing to endanger their friendship but enough to make it clear who stood a little taller in the eyes of the world. Besides, Becky still believes Erica will tire of the Tate on Sundays and Greek archaeological tours and will, one day, wish to spend her weekends cleaning out a rat cage and holidaying at the Napier Family Holiday Park.

Erica pushes the DVD into the slot. She listens for the whirr and click, picking up her notepad to watch closely. New York. A cramped Brownstone apartment, a bed in one corner and a glass of gin beside the typewriter. Anne Bancroft as the eccentric writer and passionate book lover, Helene Hanff: climbing the dark stairs with brown bags of Italian pastrami and bottles of red wine, shifting a pile of books to sit down, leaning out the shuttered window to watch lovers in the street. Muttering, drinking, bashing at an old typewriter.

Erica stops writing. She must have been seventeen when she saw this movie and it filled her with impatience for life ahead. She had left Palmerston North for a degree in English Literature and then for every great city in the world. Except she had become a temp in London – and then possibly the world's most permanent temporary, followed by a slow ascent to the giddy heights of middle-management in the NHS.

Erica tried to think. When had she lost sight of becoming a writer? There must have been a moment when she stopped taking notes, stopped watching people, one day she could pinpoint. But when? Most probably one of those ghastly drinking trips around Europe, her childhood dreams muddied in a campground on the outskirts of Paris, putting up a tent in the shadow of a public housing block.

Erica glances down at the photograph album lying open on the floor. She is being watched by an intense-looking girl with scornful eyes. Angrily, she flips the album shut.

Hi Becks

Have made a start on my new visualised life. Tell me what you think.

Client A is a best-selling literary novelist (thus allowing her to maintain both her artistic integrity and a house in Portugal). She is widely read and cognisant of world affairs, subscribing to The New Yorker and Vanity Fair (strictly for Reportage Section). Client A completes the Times cryptic crossword over

'Erica, I've been wondering, do you remember when you chundered in someone's letterbox after the DD Smash concert?'

'No.'

'I do. I still have to drive past that letterbox on crèche committee nights. We were in Grunter's Ford Escort.'

'Still don't remember.'

'That's because now you drive past things like the Victoria and Albert Museum. While you're thinking about the Elgin Marbles, I'm trying not to think about Grunter.'

'They're in the British Museum.'

'Whatever. And you know what's really tragic? Sometimes I ring the carpool to say I'll be late just so I can drive to meetings with Coldplay so loud my ears bleed.'

'You're right, that is tragic.'

Erica: some homework! I want you to prepare your short-term (3-month) goals to help realise your new life. Remember to ask yourself: how am I going to live today in order to create the tomorrow I'm committed to?

Becky is tired. Today she did an Extreme class followed by StepMax, and then the crèche manager complained about

Arabella's spotty bum. *Molluscum contagiosum*. Disgusting. 'And where do you suppose she got that?' asks Becky. She pours herself a gin. Now Bevan is in the Skyline she can officially start drinking at five while eating with the kids. She used to cook another meal when Bevan came home – as she told the mothers' group, eating together was important, a time to talk about your husband's day and strengthen the bonds of marriage through meaningful communication.

Well, that didn't work and now Bevan's idea of meaningful communication is to have the Skyline networked.

> Erica: Thought for the day: there is no such thing as failure - only results!
> And guess what? Daishen says it's time to get real clients! I have to write them up as case studies for my final project. I've already placed ads in a couple of newspapers.

Erica is making a single-serve casserole with a small can of lemon pepper tuna. She stops in astonishment to watch the ITV news. Chaos in Kensington. A fund-raising gala has been disrupted by a swarm of bees which has terrorised a string quartet and twenty Morris dancers before alighting on Peter Pan. Nigel from Erica's bee club is discussing the irresponsibility of some urban beekeepers. Were they her bees? It was difficult to tell.

Erica puts the casserole in the microwave and sits down at the computer. It seems her new life has just turned up in the form of Becky's first case study: Anna Murdoch, a Wellington writer living in Tinakori Road (practically Katherine Mansfield! says Becky). Unable to finish her novel, she has sought help in formulating and meeting her goals (isn't that soooooo amazing?). And another client, Syd, a lovely guy who works in Dispatch at the Glaxo factory and wants to take his life to the next level. Becky thinks she can help.

> P.S. Erica! Ask yourself: what did I accomplish today to help achieve my goals? What action steps will I take tomorrow?

Becky thinks about edges as she makes a Bushells Smooth Blend and reaches for the Kahlúa – just enough to take the edge off things. Funny how other people like edges: Bevan going on about cutting-edge technology and edgy software designers. This morning she found James in the bathroom conducting experiments with her pipette of Cellex-C Eye Contour Serum. Now she'll have to sand back the dent in the door, but really, she was very restrained. Ninety-two dollars a bottle! Becky feels proud to have never hit the children.

But she is having trouble connecting with her aspirations. Close your eyes, Daishen suggests, breathe deeply and allow a movie screening of your life to play out in your mind. So Becky sets her clock to five a.m. for a ten-minute mini-meditation, only Arabella hears the alarm and wanders into the bedroom just as Becky is visualising her plate of homemade cinnamon scrolls. '*Can't I have ten bloody minutes to myself?*' she yells, before remembering to take slow deep breaths and think about alternative strategies for stress.

Becky has started Syd on his goals and visualisation techniques. She detects some resistance and feels it's time to introduce her Four-Point Plan.

'Is it fair to raise his expectations of life?' says Erica.

'They're his expectations not mine.'

'But wouldn't it be kinder to say, "Look Syd, you're a nice bloke but no rocket scientist. Stick with Dispatch and go for breeding sausage dogs."'

'Of course, night classes! Everyone with a life coach goes to night classes.'

'Becky, don't you ever worry about the sort of people attracted to a life coach?'

'Fruitloops?'

'I was going to say vulnerable. Seriously, aren't you worried you might cause real harm?'

'No, we've been warned to look out for nutters. I know the signs.'

'Really? But I thought madness was one of the hardest things to diagnose? Sometimes a little knowledge can be the most dangerous.'

'Exactly, Miss Psychology 101.'

Becky completes a questionnaire that identifies her personal stress triggers as James and Arabella. Bevan comes next, followed by something called 'unrealistic personal expectations'. Daishen tells her to keep a stress log and rate her stress levels on a scale from one to five. Becky takes her work/life balance statement off the fridge and adds *I am relaxed and stress-free always.*

But she can't understand how, after a streamlining exercise that relieved her of many unnecessary duties (including parent help in the classroom and the family goldfish), she is busier than ever. She can barely keep up – but it's the scheduled ten minutes of quiet time that really does her head in. She swots up multitasking and makes a chicken and lentil casserole (fat 15g, protein 28g), freezing it into serving-size portions. Then she sits down to fill out a questionnaire. *What is complicating my life right now?*

Becky has agreed to meet Daishen in a chatroom this evening. He says quality contact time is important now she's approaching graduation. She tells him she's having trouble with role-modelling and he suggests a rebranding exercise. Does her image reflect her true self? Becky agrees to email some photos so Daishen can do an image audit.

Erica looks at her bedroom curtains. They're almost worn through but her landlady disagrees. Erica feels too old to be renting – it's demeaning to plead for new curtains. And yet eight years ago it had been luxury to rent this place – no more putting up with flatmates, or worse still, their boyfriends. She had found this house the same week she found a strange bloke asleep behind the sofa and that her bowl of Milk Oaties, soaking overnight in the fridge, had been scoffed.

Now these flatmates were back home with a mortgage. Like Becky, who had been so excited to show off her new house, an ugly roughcast bungalow with a Skyline sleep-out and a wetback. Erica had thought this some sort of spider but no, apparently a wetback was something to do with the fireplace and what Becky had absolutely always wanted. Funny. Becky had never mentioned a wetback in London.

Erica had looked about the small kitchen with the egg-stained high chair and found herself thinking, oddly enough, of Becky's mother, Claudia Lockyard. She could now appreciate that it *was* an accomplishment to live a life of style and distinction, that to be the first woman in Palmerston North with curtain swags was not to be scoffed at. And now Becky was going on about the joys of owning a fully lined sleep-out with carpet tiles.

They had gone for a walk along the cul-de-sac, Erica pushing Arabella's pram while Becky and James stopped to peer between every fence picket. Erica could feel her life shrinking in the afternoon heat, she was being suffocated by the nothingness and staring window eyes of the suburban street. Trying not to panic, Erica had tried to calculate the time in London and what her friends might be doing now. Anything to remind her a world continued outside this timeless non-existence. How had Becky's life come to this?

Becky had rung soon after, buoyed by the success of Erica's visit. 'So when are you coming back home to live?'

'Um. When I'm diagnosed with a terminal disease?'

'Ha-ha.' Becky had been pissed off but Erica wasn't joking. She loved London but she didn't want to die there.

Becky is up early to make cinnamon scrolls – the mothers' group is arriving at ten. She cleans the house, gets James to school, sweeps the path and manages a five-minute mini-meditation before the doorbell goes. Thank goodness Maxine's had a minor haemorrhage and can't join them. Talk turns to a baby discovered left in a hot car for three hours and everyone is aghast. Becky feels light-headed and has the urge to giggle. Dreadful, they murmur, helping themselves to more cinnamon scrolls.

Erica is depressed about her curtains and now she's having problems at work. Her recreation advisor is leaving just as Get Moving! is to be launched into several rest homes. It seems he would prefer to clean the locker rooms at Highbury than coach the elderly in the intricacies of carpet bowls. Erica finds that she can't really blame him.

Today Becky is feeling great. She has already met her targets and there might even be time to start on the garden. She is in control, achieving her goals, meeting her work/life balance statement. Everything is perfect except the children refused to eat their chicken and lentil casserole last night and she threw both plates against the wall and thumped Arabella on the head with a frozen meal. She can't recall anything but a sick, shaky feeling afterwards. Arabella is fine but Becky may have to touch up the wall. Still, she is a good painter and now she's stopped watching television there are so many more hours to achieve things. Becky rates her stress levels today at three. *Remember, Becky: make every day count!*

Daishen says it's only natural to feel stressed and she must look for ways to relax and how about a walk along the beach at sunset? But Becky doesn't feel like a drive to Foxton. Daishen suggests a long soak in a bath surrounded by candles. Of course she's stressed without Bevan. Doesn't she know lovemaking releases pheromones that relax the body and promote a sense of well-being? Becky must learn to pamper herself. *Write down five ways you would choose to pamper yourself and schedule them into your diary.*

Becky starts on her case studies. It seems Syd has read *Feel the Fear and Do It Anyway* but is still in Dispatch. Becky suspects complacency – Syd must be encouraged out of his comfort zone, has he considered a triathlon? Syd emails back. He is twenty-two stone with dicky hips. 'Oh,' says Becky, 'then try balloon tennis.' Honestly, she's getting tired of Syd and his dreary life.

Thankfully Anna Murdoch is doing much better, meeting all her writing targets and even sending a synopsis to a publisher. 'You won't believe it, Erica – her book is on bees!'

'But bees have been done, there are heaps of bee novels and all published within the past five years. I've read them.'

'Oh. Do you think I should tell her?'

'She must know.'

But Anna Murdoch did not know, nor did she appreciate Becky imposing her self-limiting beliefs. Becky apologised and said there was always room in the world for another bee book. 'But Erica,' says Becky, 'listen to a journal entry of her typical day. It's fantastic – you've got to model yourself on her:

> 'I live in an old wooden cottage covered with rambling roses. There are piles of book everywhere and my writing study is upstairs. Sometimes I sit at the window looking down on the people who pass along Tinakori Road and invent their back-stories. I start each day with a cup of tea and the crossword. I usually work until two, stopping only for a freshly brewed coffee. In the afternoon I walk through the botanical gardens, sometimes taking the cable car down to visit a gallery. My evenings are spent reading.'

'So how does she earn an income?' asks Erica.

'Who knows? But tell me, with a life like that, how come she's never been published?'

'Maybe she's a crap writer.'

'Erica, that's very self-limiting.'

'No, it's honest. Do you ever ask your clients to be honest with themselves?'

Becky makes a note to ask Daishen about self-honesty.

Arabella has been swearing at crèche and the manager is angry. 'Well, where do you think she learnt that?' says Becky, before frogmarching her daughter out the door, a thumb and finger inserted firmly into either side of Arabella's neck. The next day there are two purple bruises and Becky feels sick as she dresses her in a Tiny Tots pink skivvy. But Arabella is happy; she loves pink. Becky makes up for it by scheduling baking into her diary and that afternoon they make fairy cakes together. *Remember, Becky: give yourself a pat on the back!*

Bevan has seen the Visa bill and is really pissed off. ReInventYourself? What the hell's that? Things are pretty tight at the moment, Rebecca, what with you ringing London every five minutes. Becky drives to the gym with the stereo turned off, repeating her mantra: *I now attract prosperity into my life. I now attract prosperity into my life.*

Erica wonders what book Anna is reading and Becky promises to ask. She rings back later that week: *Snow Falling on Cedars.*

'You're kidding? Anything else?'

'*The Shipping News*?'

'Oh dear.'

'Well I liked it, especially the movie. And there's…'

'Let me guess. *Captain Corelli's Mandolin.*'

'*White Teeth* actually. She couldn't really get into *Captain Corelli.*'

'Becky, that's a book club reading list from eight years ago. She's a fraud.'

Erica looks out the back window. Her backyard looks even more ugly without the hive. No wonder the bees buggered off, she thinks, as the Heathrow Express screams past. She imagines them buzzing happily among the daisies in Kensington Gardens – next thing they're in a field of flowering manuka. The pohutukawa are in bloom and Erica is standing in a paddock looking down over a sandy bay, her hives dotted about like little crooked towers. Another train screams past and Erica looks at her watch. She's got a steering group meeting in an hour.

Becky has told Daishen she isn't coping. He says he's looking at her photo (the one in the white Nike tracksuit!) and she's looking great – really great. Self-care is so important. He suggests she keep a food diary to watch the mid-afternoon snacking, and don't forget to rehydrate. *Remember, Becky! Schedule your workouts in your diary and make them non-negotiable appointments!* Also, he mentions casually, she should consult with her personal trainer over the butt exercises – looks like she could do with a little help.

'I'm having some problems with Syd,' Becky tells Erica. 'Did you know the Glaxo factory closed ten years ago?'

'No. Does Syd?'

'Who knows, who cares? And now Anna turns out to be Susan-from-Johnsonville with a good job at Inland Revenue.'

'A fraud, I knew it.'

'According to Daishen it's a good example of self-actualisation, otherwise known as "fake it till you make it". He thinks Anna–Susan is making really good progress.'

'She sounds like a loser to me.'

'I know.'

'Still, she had a good imagination.'

'She watched *84 Charing Cross Road*.'

Erica switches on the computer and does a Google search on Waiheke Island. She feels a buzz of excitement. That's it! Exactly where she saw her bees. Sandy bays fringed with flowering pohutukawa, green paddocks and small winding roads. She links onto a real estate site, scrolling excitedly through the properties. She stops, shocked, staring with horror. She could buy an entire house in Hounslow for that sort of money.

Becky is afraid to turn on the computer. The emails from Daishen are coming every twenty minutes – he must be up all night. *How's the seven-day time tracker going? What about the personal contract? He loves hearing from her – has she considered becoming a writer?* Becky is so tired and Arabella needs her fairy costume fixed for ballet tomorrow and now Daishen is becoming angry. *Why is she ignoring him? Why wasn't she in the chatroom tonight? He's looking at her photo all the time. All the time. Is this all the thanks he gets? All that help and she's giving him the big freeze? Write, you bitch. Write.*

Erica lies in bed and stares at the ceiling. She can hear the scream of an approaching train. It passes, clattering like the flicking tail of a movie reel, sending flashes of shuttered light across the room. Could she really be a writer? But how to start? (Becky would suggest a night class, of course.) There was little to give her cause for hope – her teenage scribblings had been awful and it was all very well to say she had years of experience – but of what? Menial office work and middle-management. Hah. She can see it now: a literary thriller about a policy analyst. Erica rolls over and shuts her eyes, she can hear another train coming, *clattering like the flicking tail of a movie reel...*

Becky knocks on the door of the Skyline. Bevan is on the computer and he looks up, surprised. He follows her into the kitchen and turns on the computer, taking time to read the emails, the back of his neck turning red. It's disgusting, he says. How did Becky meet this guy? He's insane. Bevan squares his shoulders in preparation for battle, armed with an artillery of firewalls and ISP filters, to defend his wife's honour and the sanctity of his family home.

Becky busies herself at the sink feeling a thrill of alarm and wishing Bevan would be angry more often. He turns, triumphant. He has installed a protective system to keep the dirty bugger out. It seems there never was a ReInventYourself! – except Daishen, of course, and Becky has lost out on a qualification and fifteen hundred US dollars. She nods, trying to look upset. The truth is, Becky is relieved. She feels wonderfully, extraordinarily free. She rips her work/life balance statement from the fridge and shoves it in the bin.

By the way, Becky asks casually, would you like a wine? She's picked up an Aussie shiraz from New World today. Bevan nods and she reaches for the wine glasses. So anyway, Bevan, how are things going? He looks away. Not so good, Becky. Turns out there are no beaches in New Mexico – and no Pink Batts in the Skyline either. It's starting to get cold out there, Becks.

Erica! Someone at our mothers' group mentioned a piece of land near the old Longburn Freezers. A couple of acres. There are some pine trees which should give some protection as it can get pretty windy on the flats, otherwise it's mostly gorse so I'm sure manuka will grow. Your bees will love it! What do you think?

Erica stares at the green glowing screen and slowly shakes her head. She doesn't know what to think any more.

THE GREAT
WHERE ARE WE

BRIAN TURNER

The Great Where Are We

When gods were young
This wind was old.
            – Edward Thomas

Find a hollow like a flue
on the hillside
and sprawl and watch
the dramas unfold
in the great where are we,
the sky.

Then listen to the wind,
that's older
than Methuselah,
singing the songs
earth intuits in us.

Sadness and Shadow

The one known as The Leader said
If we can discern the difference
between sadness and shadow
we'll have unlocked the doors to peace.

So they trooped off into the hills
to a hut at the head of a tussocky valley
with snarls of matagouri in the gulleys
and vast shields of scree like grey-blue tunics
on the mountains all round.

And there they stayed. The sun shone
without libation, the wind blew *whoo*
under the edges of the roofing iron.
On nights when the moon was bright
mica sparkled in schist by the river.

In winter they went to bed early
leaving the fire to burn slowly
through the night, a dervish,
and the river muttered and shrank.
Mice scurried along rafters and squeaked.

Weeks went by. No one wanted to be first
to say it was time to go home. One
by one they died forlorn, unenlightened,
wondering where, exactly, they'd
come from, and if anyone was still there
wittering on about free trade

and indigenous rights, prostitution,
rugby and the demise of *Friday Flash*.

Bewildereds couldn't understand why
technological *advances* hadn't solved
age-old questions, removed dilemma,
or why even the brightest people stumbled
when faced with the conflict between
personal expression and social obligation.

Eventually the sole survivor
walked out of the hills
but couldn't find one familiar face,
so she returned to the hut
in the mountains and buried
the remains of her friends,
and she lay down beside sadness
and shadow and waited to hear
the lilting sounds of peace on the wind.

Sky Lessons

Learn to differentiate or don't join the class.
Don't speak of clouds but of cirrus, stratus,

cumulus, nimbus ... their shapes cape-like or plumed
and turned by the wind in updrafts impertinent;

note their hues piqued by the clarity of the light
matching moods of the day, and the absence

of competitors that infatuate. Theirs the greatest
cathedral of all, stratus and cirrus lined up

like pews, nimbus like priests glowering in the nave,
cumulus towering white as angels above the altar.

Worship skies, then, where the numinous does not
elude us, where no dark, water-borne Charon waits.

Holy Music
(after Rilke)

Where does harmony go
when the rain in your heart beats hard,
        when the tall dry late summer grasses

leached of green, sway
as if to music only they can hear,
        as if to the sounds of water deep

in the ground? If you were an instrument,
what would you be? A harp on a hillside
        in a land of perennially long summer evenings?

A cello in an arena packed
with earthenware urns? A piano whose keys
        reflected light like shingle dancing

in an alpine stream? Holy, do not lament
your lack of desire while you can still
        hear music that is holy, that induces

the piety that insists life must
not be the enemy of art, and will not
        transport you to some even stranger place.

Say you are, because you were.

Seasonal Gales

When you say that life is brief,
sometimes very, and often brutal,
few disagree, and fewer still
appear to wander off to reflect
on raucous scenes from another life,
as far as you can tell.

And when a visitor riding
the Central Otago Rail Trail
spots you in the local store
and asks if you are 'an identity'
you're tempted to say
apart from having one you've no idea.

Reminiscence is progress that has
few subscribers for going back's
just too hard, which is why
you haven't the faith to shake
the decree about the need to put
the past behind and move on.

For now there's a wild gale
blowing out of the northwest,
the oak's all heavy breathing,
and the red-berried rowan's
as alarming as stigmata.
All who live here know

the sort of wind that flings
bits and pieces of willow across
the road and strips topsoil
off raked paddocks, the wind that returns,
like anger and ridicule and other storms
that keep on rolling in.

Home Hills, February
(for Grahame Sydney)

It's said that autumn's already on its way
    by those who know about such things
and yet, truly, few things matter less
        this afternoon, a few miles up the road
from Hills Creek where Baxter spent
    holidays in his youth, dived into the race
and swam through the culvert
        under the road where tree roots
could easily have trapped him.

It must have been 60 years, or more, ago,
    when several houses squatted there
and trees were smaller and fewer,
        and the sod cottage nearest
the main road corner wasn't used – though
    who really knows? – by a foxy 70-year-old
and a younger woman who looks, locals say,
        barely a quarter his age.

Today, there's just me, Jacquie the aged golden lab
    whose coat is like bleached tussock,
and the painter Grahame Sydney. The Hawkduns
        to the north, Home Hills and their easy curves
to the west, and a few fluffy clouds
    primping in the distance above Moa Creek
and the Poolburn's sprawling hills trending south
        at the far end the Ida Valley.

A warm and gentle wind puffs intermittently,
    flies buzz, and, ambling – in my case hobbling,
due to stitches in my abdomen – one needs to
        beware of lancing spaniards, whose
late flower-stems are bowed and tatty
    like the standards of a beaten army.

Syd's spotted the yards, iron woolshed, bunkhouses
    and a three-roomed roughcast cookhouse
whose long wooden table seats at least twelve.
        He says, 'I see several paintings here,'
as he lifts his sketch pad, clip board
    and small red canvas folding stool from his vehicle
and sets out to make some pencil drawings.
        He finds a spot among late dandelion,
purple-headed thistles, stunted matagouri,
    rabbit scrapes, sheep shit, dry grey plonks
of cattle dung, clumps of tussock, and pink
        and white clover gone to seed. Old iron
and rotting timber is clamped in the wavier grass ...
    so much to comprehend in all
that is past its best and yet not past.

An elderberry girds part of one wall
    of the woolshed – used mainly for crutching
now, and storing saddlery for the hacks
        that graze undisturbed nearby –

and delicate willows sprout from a soak
    30 metres away. Inside the shed,
and bunkrooms, walls and floors and wire
        mattresses are streaked with bird-droppings.
Brooms and scrapers are propped against
    holding pens; hooks hang from rafters.
Concrete piping lies against a wall; cupboards
       and safes are missing doors,
windows are broken, gappy as memory.
    Grey and white gulls' feathers flitter
around the base of a drum half full of stretchy tar.

I stroke the muzzle of a chestnut hack
    that sidles up to the fence
behind the woolshed, while the dog,
       belly wet and dirty from digging up
a hedgehog's nest, slobbers and sniffles,
    collapses panting in the shade
of a tussock. Birds chitter and fuss
       but can't suppress the noise
this sprawling country makes.

'I won't be long,' Syd says, 'just one more drawing.'
    For once we are not men behaving sadly
or badly, but gladly. And looking north
       towards the head of the Manuherikia
the farther off the bluer the hills become.

Same Old Same Old

Across the valley, at the bottom of the fluted clay cliffs,
a big wind is funnelling out of the gorge
but you can't hear it from here. The willows
nodding like supplicants tell us how fresh
it must be, so here…what is it like here?
There's a cloud like a marquee above us
full of upended tables and chairs
and the children have lost their enthusiasm
for candy floss and each others' snickery
and spite. The bride, inconsiderate slut,
is an hour late – but you get that –
for the biggest mistake of her life,
the groom's drunk on Coruba, his nana's
refusing to vote National for the first time
in her blinkered life, and both sets of parents
are saying their worst fears have been confirmed.
In other words, same old same old.

Across the valley is where you'd sooner be
in the place where annually misogynists'
and manhaters' conventions are set up
on opposite sides of the river, and Charon's
slinky longboat plies back and forth every night.

Hills

Someone said the hills
were slumbering in the heat.
Another said
they were meditating.
My friend said
they were talking crap,
those two, that hills
were there for tussock
and bracken and gentians
to grow on. They all
had an idea about
the hills. I said
we're all hills too
and that they would
watch us with amusement
until we died
at which point there would be
no argument
as to who was
or was not a hill.

Ida Valley, January

This is the time
   when the windows
      rattle in the nor'wester,
         scotch thistles prepare to seed
      and the lucerne's waving acres
   of violet and green. Young thrushes
and blackbirds risk their lives
   on the ground. My neighbour's cat,
      gingery, austere, is meant
         to protect the raspberries
      from the avians and doesn't.
   I go to bed only half-pie
sound in mind and body
   and the mind starts roving,
      wars with sleep, always
         finds something else
to take issue with.

March Ride

There are peaks in the sky
above the peaks in the north and west,
St Bathans lording it, the Hawkduns
scuffed yet seemly as always.

The wind and sun and rain
shapes them all. At the Moa Creek corner
I turn into the wind
and set off for home, watch

herons flung sideways
like blue-grey rags, see ardent shivers
skelter across a silvered pond
and listen for cadence

in lulls between gusts in the gale
that's lifting soil off ploughed paddocks
and sending it south
in plumes like smoke.

On Top of the World
(for Kila Hepi)

The days seem longer all of a sudden
now that August's here
and inventions become realities
ingrained.

Riding between Wedderburn
and Hills Creek we're on top
of the world, my young friend Kila
and I, the clouds like white drapery
spilling down the mountains,
and the sun's like acclamation
strobing the downs. And the angels
in their white dresses
kick their bangled heels
and dabble their feet
in the ever blue blue.

It seems that the purer
the air the greater one's ardour.
We stop and listen for the songs
of air and water and I swear
I heard the rapt sounds
of angels singing, not of Paradise lost
but Paradise now.

Hawks in a Gale

Hawks pendulum in the gale.
They're looking for field mice,
young rabbits, birds, anything
dead or alive, and their flight's
panic-punctuated grace
fine-tuning their desperation.

Cold Place

We came to a place
shaded for all
but an hour a day,

a place of wet black
rock and scree
and water devoid

of hue, a place
where the wind
was bitterly cold

and icicles fused.
The stockman
drawled it was

no place for men,
so cold we wouldn't
be back. It was

said in such a tone
he expected us
to believe him.

The Vernacularies

Beware of strangers, the children are told.
In other words, just about everyone,
the message being it's not worth
trying to find a saint
among the legions of sinners,
time's too precious.
                    Or so the old joker
who lives in a shack up the road reckons,
says he's in the dark most of the time
though he's working on it. 'I'm
up with the vernacularies,' he says
with a grin like a crack in schist.
'I'm trying to shed some light
on the meaning of life.'
                    My mother
would have approved of his manners,
said *there's a lesson for you*
and reminded me of the need to
take people as you find them
and don't go looking for the dark side
for that's where the spiders are.

She could have said light and dark
go together like sweet and sour,
but she didn't. You can put her
tact down to her age
and a certain intrinsic female poise
that goes with being *a good woman*
all her life, someone
unspectacularly spectacular.

You can make a pact
with someone like that
though there's no guarantee
it will get you to heaven.

Presbyterian Support Services

It seems a wan place to be
perhaps because you're surrounded by discards
and you're aware that some would say
you could do with sprucing up yourself…
which, by certain standards of the day –
what others are there? – is true.

The down-at-heel often seem
stripped of pride in their appearance
was what your spic father intoned,
asserting they lacked that cluck of self-esteem,
and though money's sure as hell
not everything, what do you do
when you haven't got much of it
except rummage about in an op shop
where there's more hush than hurrah?

You guess there's no pat answer
and while most of the clothes
have a lot of life left in them
they are dulled by their failure
to disclose the dramas
they were party to. Not only that,
you're nagged by the thought
that the last time
you bought a pair of jeans here
a female friend wondered if you knew
they were *really* a woman's
and you ought to have known that
by the waist measurement
and the size of the arse.

Conduct

To remember is to disclose,
A woman violinist believes.

Her music ignites, retrieves
lost links that presuppose

There were very good reasons
to put a career in music

ahead of a family, seasons
down on the farm, the fabric

convention sternly refused
leaving scores bowed, bemused.

Dictionaries of National Biography

My father's father, quirky
and inquisitive till the end,
was the first to tell me

you never stop learning.
Well, I don't know about you
but this fine December morning

I learned that Krishna Menon
was deemed 'devastatingly'
attractive to women, Jane Austen

showed few signs of having
much of a sense of humour,
Florence Nightingale, the Lady

with the Lamp, was 'a good mimic'
and Thomas Batty, the first man
to train an elephant to stand

on its head, died in a lunatic
asylum. Also, the not always grand
Duke of York succumbed

to dropsy. So what about me,
then, as 62 approaches?
As my father caustically said

each time he saw me
for months before he died,
I need a haircut.

Vane

Nostalgia's a weather vane
        that veers from fact to fiction,
    imaginary to real, what's

perceived as such; and as such
        it's the big *if only* linked
    to the sad *what if?* It's

what you never stop asking,
        what splinters happiness,
    hobbles the wish to be

oh so precise, robust, explicit.

Mailbox

The lilac's finery's flawless.
No wind disturbs it,
nothing's wild in the heavens,

what's temporary's in tune
with temperament, and that's
just as well for a letter

I wished I hadn't opened
lies on the dining table
like a crumpled napkin…

and my neighbour, on her way
to feed the dogs, tells me
something everyone agrees with,

it's time we had some rain.

The Spade

Cleaves sod cleanly,
glints like a knife-blade

when hosed down
and left to dry in the sun.

Cuts the roots off tubers neatly,
deals to the edges of lawns,

doubles the number of worms,
scrapes mud off paths and boots,

smirks when put away
in the corner of the shed.

CHASING FIREFLIES

PHOEBE WRIGHT

My father believed in Fate. When he was ten he let a coin decide whether he would ever speak to his sister again. His sister's name was Dot. Tails yes, heads no, on the side only if Dot could guess the number he was thinking. It came down tails, but then Dot refused to speak to my father for weeks anyway. She thought he didn't care enough for her affections to make a proper decision.

He did care, he just believed in Fate.

My father bought 1,963 lottery tickets in his lifetime. I know because he could never throw anything away. I know because I spent an afternoon counting them.

When he was fifteen, he fell in love. She had slanting eyes, freckled knees, milk-coffee-coloured hair braided down her back, a smile that made him think of dappled sunlight. In his diary, an adolescent scrawl: 'Today, I saw the most beautiful girl in the whole wide world!' And after he had lain awake all night: 'Yesterday, I fell in love!'

He waited. He waited faithfully. He walked by her house, but on the other side of the street. He chose all her classes at school, discovered a passion for biology he never knew he had, but made no attempt to sit near her. He waited patiently. He spent hours watching her. He eavesdropped on her friends, basked in each new, glorious titbit of information. He learned she was stubborn, but blushed easily. She wore a cross about her neck, and habitually pulled on the chain at the back as if to make the golden pendant more conspicuous. She loved sour fruit and weak tea. Once she won a swimming race, but was so embarrassed at being looked at by so many in her bathing suit that she never raced again. She bit her nails.

He waited for years. But as Fate had it, she never so much as glanced at him.

He learned the viola so he could join the orchestra in which she was first flute. He memorised his music so he could spend every rehearsal watching her across the room, through the strings of the harpist's harp. She might have noticed him if he had chosen a louder instrument. She might have looked up upon the flare of a silver trumpet, smiled through the harp strings. Things might have happened sooner. He might not have had to build the world's smallest coffin, he could have become everything and given Gran something to believe in.

What can I say? My father chose the viola. My father believed in Fate.

Memory

I am looking into the fire. Rough hands are braiding my hair down my back. He gently tosses one long black braid over my shoulder, begins the other side. I am safe.

'Do you want to hear a story?'

I nod. He loses his place, starts again, which is what I want, more than the story.

'Once upon a time there was a boy.'

The fire crackles.

'What did he look like?'

'Why does that matter?'

'Because.'

'Because what?'

'Nothing.'

'Once upon a time there was a boy. One day he saw the most beautiful girl in the whole wide world.'

'Was her hair as long as mine?'

'I don't mean that sort of beautiful.'

'Can you plait tighter?'

'I don't want to hurt you.'

'Dad?'

'What, honey?'

'Why do all your stories end sad?' With Dad, that's the sort of thing that gets you a hug, which is what I want, more than anything. He smells like sweat, but also like my mother, who smells like lemon blossom, which smells like sadness.

'I'll try and make this one happy, okay?' I put my hand in his jacket pocket. It is big, because he has big hands. I feel fluff, a broken match, two old Lotto tickets.

'Okay.'

The people who most want to believe in God are the ones who can't. My mother has had herself baptised seven times. Her adoptive parents were atheists; she hasn't spoken to them since she was eighteen. She prays every day, or at least kneels and moves her lips. She went to Jerusalem, posted a blank slip of paper in the Wailing Wall, because she could not bring herself to write 'exist'. She will be buried with that chain about her clammy neck. When she is one with the earth, it will remain, suspended in soil for all eternity.

My mother could have stayed in England and become a nun. She could have lived a happy, holy lie. My father would have painfully concluded it wasn't what Fate had in mind. I would not be.

My mother could have stayed in England and become a nun. Her lie might have saved lives. But after they graduated (with identical qualifications, although she had better grades), they both coincidentally signed up for field work experience with the same entomology research programme. My father no doubt saw this as a promising sign. They spoke for the first time ten thousand feet above the Atlantic Ocean. He thought he might cry when he walked up the aisle to see her skim-reading the New Testament next to his empty seat. She thought he was strange because during their seven hours and forty-five minutes in the air he never once stopped smiling.

Thought
I'm here, but I'm not ready to be here. So I watch, so I wait, so I write.

Time does strange things in airports. Uncomfortable

benches are draped with travellers seizing sleep at all hours. Clocks race past precious parting moments, yet ticking hands linger for those who await returning loves. Tears, joyful and grieving, wash these crossroads of time; sweeping away words that were too awkward to utter, gathering us all in the current, scattering us across the world.

A guard is looking at me. He has dark glasses on, but I know he's looking at me. I close my notebook (leaving my parents suspended above the ocean halfway to America), slide it into my bag, which is practically empty (how do people fill those ridiculous wheeled suitcases?), zip up, strap up.

I exit the grey timewarp through sliding doors, glance back, is he still watching? I take a breath, step out into the warm darkness, am immediately swallowed up by the steamy Italian night. Ready or not...

My grandfather believes in everything.

He believes in ghosts and fairytales, we once spent weeks planning a trip to Atlantis.

He believes in miracles and happy endings, he is every bit as comfortable in a church, mosque, any temple, as he is in the synagogue.

He believes in lies, even his own. Especially his own.

He once told me the midnight-blue rug with the silver tassels was a flying carpet, but he said he wouldn't tell me the magic word until I grew up.

He believes in magic, and my father, who could have been everything, and not via decomposition.

He believes in God and himself, though he sometimes gets them mixed up.

He believes that the Messiah will come, sooner rather than later.

He believes that the world was made of circles, his rainbows never end.

He believes that he can make my grandmother happy again, more than anyone ever believed anything.

Memory

Thirteen, sitting at the bus shelter outside school, rain, I swear it used to rain harder when we were kids, we could have been sitting under a waterfall, it could have been raining bullets, nothing can touch us. I'm painting Wendy's nails blue, we're laughing so hard, there didn't have to be a reason back then, why do we have to grow up? We're talking about Danny; we were all in love with him in those days. He overdosed before we turned sixteen, never grew up, he'll always be a kid running on the soccer field, smiling under the mud splatters, smiling, ears cold and pink listening to our cheers, when did he stop smiling, why do we have to grow up?

'He–y, who's the old guy with the weird hat?' She points, a drop lands on the nail I just finished. The world's tiniest splash. Beautiful. Am I the only person who notices things like that?

Julia giggles, it sounds like the fire crackling.

'He's smiling at us, *dodgy*, innit?'

'He doesn't have an umbrella or anything!'

'Maybe he, y'know, escaped from an *institution* or something…'

Grandad's waving across the street, sodden kippah slipping to one side of his bald skull.

'Chaya!' He's laughing. They all look at me. 'Chaya! This is the great flood all over again, no? Never fear, my own personal ark is parked just round the block!'

'Oh my *god*, Chaya, do you, like, *know* him?'

I want to write that I said: '*Yes*, that beautiful person standing in the rain is the best grandad in the whole wide world, and he's mine, mine, mine!'

I mutter 'kinda', step out into the rain so they won't see my tears, walk slowly across the street wishing to be run over, don't speak to him the whole way home.

What can I say? I'm sorry?

My grandmother didn't believe in anything. She did once, but then lived through a terrible time, in which many people stopped believing in God, and fair enough, but she was never one to do things by halves.

'Trees?' My grandfather asked her. 'Stars?'

'No.'

'Rain? Laughter?'

'No.'

'Books? Water lilies?'

'No.'

'Music? Memories?'

'No.'

'Poland? Happiness?'

'No.'

His eyes brimmed. 'Love? Me?'

'I wish...' She stared out the window, grey eyes, grey buildings, grey sky. 'I wish...'

Thought

I'm in Italy. A thought indeed.

The street is crowded. Rain-wet cobblestones feel strange under my sneakers. A cacophony of Italian fills the night around me, is there a more beautiful language? Florence. Is there a more beautiful city?

The stars are out. I can smell something spicy, I want to laugh, how can this even be the same planet?

A man near a fountain is selling fruit from a cart. He shouts his wares to the passers-by. He catches my eye, plucks a single green grape, holds it up.

'*Grappoli dolci, Signorina!*' He squeezes until juice trickles between his fingers, throws the crushed grape over his shoulder, kisses fingers with gusto. I'm sold. I point, wave some notes from my pocket. It's more than any sane person would pay for grapes, but tonight I don't care.

'*Grappoli*, um, *Signore.*'

'*Inglese?* Yes, most best fruit for you today, *Signorina!*' He dumps the grapes into my arms, whisks the money from my outstretched hand, counts quickly.

'*Grazie,*' I say. He looks up from the money, laughs.

'For a friend like you I think we have also this most best fruit!' He gives me an orange. Before I can thank him again, he is bargaining loudly with the man behind me, slipping my money into the back pocket of his jeans.

My hotel room is two floors up and right across the road from the Cathedral, the Duomo, how did I manage to afford this? I lean over my dusty window sill, in awe, eating sweet, seedless grapes, watching the people below me, happy. I'm here to try to forget why I'm here. It's working.

My lips are dry from the flight (does that happen to everyone?), my smile stretches, hurts, but I can't stop, I let the juice drip down my chin, happy, I'm somewhere no one in my family has ever been before...

But then my smile flickers, I look over at the red notebook lying open on my narrow bed, realise I've brought them with me.

Will the past ever be over?

In America, they became colleagues, friends, lovers. At least, he was a lover. She was just homesick, lonely.

Every time he picked her up, he gave her a new compliment.

'Your hair looks beautiful tonight.'

'Thank you.'

'You are even more beautiful than your eyes.'

'Thanks.'

'Your nose is beautiful.'

'My nose?'

'Your nose.'

He wanted to take her to the Grand Canyon, skating on a frozen lake, to the prairies to read poetry in the middle of nowhere. But she always wanted to just drink tea because she was homesick, and talk about ordinary things, because she was lonely.

'You make that colour beautiful.'

'Don't you mean it makes me look beautiful?'

He smiled and shook his head.

She plucked at her sleeve. 'Brings out my eyes, or something?'

'I don't mean that sort of beautiful.'

She laughed, pulled on the chain at the back of her neck. 'I like you.'

And she did, just never enough.

Memory

Standing in the kitchen, halfway into my uniform, it's still dark outside; I can feel the chill of the dark–blue tiles through my socks.

'Mum?'

'Yes, Chaya?'

'Tell me a story.' Her smooth hands find a stray wisp of hair; work it back into the braid.

'Say please next time. Just a short one though, all right?'

'Okay.'

'Once upon a time, there was a girl, whose life was saved by a butterfly.'

'Was she like Thumbelina?'

'Sort of.'

'What colour was…'

'Do you want to hear the story or not?'

'Sorry.'

My back is to her, but I know she's pursing her lips.

'How did it save her?'

'She was drowning, and it rescued her.'

'Did she marry it?'

'People can't marry butterflies.'

'But if she was little, like Thumbelina…'

'Still.'

'Mum?'

'Yes, Chaya?'

'Can you plait looser?'

'I don't want it to come undone. And please remember to say please, Chaya.'

'Mum?'

'What, Chaya?'

'Can I have a little brother, please?' My mother has the most beautiful laugh in the whole wide world. She pecks my ear with her lips.

'We'll see.'

My grandparents met in a displaced persons camp in the American zone of Germany in 1946. It was crowded and smelly. Everyone had lost everyone; they were all mourning, all searching, largely in vain. Most people were walking skeletons, but they were alive. My grandfather was emaciated, his hair thinning prematurely. He had lost everything but his diary and his hope.

Winter thawed, teachers and doctors were flown in from America. At night, people would cry out in their sleep, wake sweating, screaming. Some would do so the rest of their lives. But by day, some sort of normality was returning. The whole world was gradually waking up from its nightmare. Strangers sometimes made eye contact, smiled again, slowly, it hurt at first. They made small talk in line for the latrine. People glanced at their reflections once more. In his diary, my grandfather wrote: 'From the ashes comes a hope fiercer than the fire. We are learning to live again.'

One cool, dry morning in spring, he stood in line for his ration of potatoes. He watched a group of skinny children play a jump-rope game, bare feet stirring up dust. They were laughing, chanting the same words he had chanted a million years ago. Others in the line watched, smiled, clapped. The woman behind him began to sob. It sounded like a wounded animal crying. He offered her an arm to lean on.

'It is all right, madam. You see, the children can laugh again, it is all right.' She wore a thick scarf over her head, and was hunched like an old woman, but when she looked up, he saw she was so very young, terribly young, they both were.

'It will be all right.'

My grandfather had lost everything but his diary and his hope.

My grandmother had lost everything.

Thought

I love waking up and having to remember where I am. Rather, I love that for once who I am comes first.

Nine flights of steep stone steps to reach the breakfast room; my coffee feels well earned. I sit by the window; see blue skies, a street coming to life below. I warm my hands on the mug; feel the sunlight on my eyelids. Good to be alive.

I'll climb the Duomo today.

There is a basket of blue potpourri in the hotel's only toilet, possibly an apology for the fact that it doesn't flush. I shove a couple of crisped petals into the pocket of my jeans. I'm trying not to believe in karma.

Later, I climb worn stone steps inside the wall of the great Cathedral. The space is narrow, the light dim. Who made these steps? How long ago?

The steps go on and on, were the builders trying to reach heaven itself? All I can see is the rather large derrière of the American tourist plodding along four steps above me. I try not to let it kill the mood.

We reach the level of the paintings around the inner dome. I thankfully slip around the American woman, who is fighting for air and loudly telling her sweaty husband that they should, like, install an elevator around here.

I've seen these paintings in books. Gory, larger-than-life murals of Hell's occupants loom down at me; fire, pitchforks, Satan himself. The face of a sinner is almost close enough to touch. She screams as a pitchfork is plunged into her back. I can hear her. She's been screaming for centuries, can't she ever be forgiven? I hurry on, suddenly desperate for fresh air. I don't believe in Hell.

It's windy on top; I'm still not used to having short hair. Beyond the rail, the great dome curves away, terracotta roofs stretch for miles to the faint grey hills on the horizon. Florence is at my feet. I eat my orange. Our guide warns me not to litter, so I put the peel in the pocket of the red coat I borrowed from my mother. A lottery ticket, a list:

Happiness of memories
Sadness of remembering
Happiness of stars
Sadness of knowing stars are getting further away
Happiness of laughter
Sadness of laughter
Happiness of being praised (love)
Sadness of knowing you don't deserve it
Happiness of sails on the horizon (hope)
Sadness of sunken ships
Happiness of moths
Sadness of butterflies
Happiness of collecting chestnuts
Sadness of might-have-been
Happiness of rain
Sadness of rainbows

She never fell in love with him. The only things she ever wanted were to believe in God, and love my father. She tried, she really did.

When the opportunity arose for some of their team to travel to South America, she took it without telling him. The selected group was to be at the receiving end of a 'Mark and Recapture' scheme aiming to measure the population and survival rate of the world's largest butterfly migration. He read her name among those listed on a noticeboard in the lab. My father and his colleagues remaining in North America would capture and 'mark' five thousand of the millions of butterflies before the migration. The method was to scrape off a small area of the wing scales, and replace them with a tiny piece of paper. The team in South America would then recapture five thousand of the millions of butterflies that completed the migration; from the number of these that were marked they could calculate the approximate population.

My father read her name from a noticeboard. Several days later, he discovered a message on his phone. About sixty seconds of her breathing, and then the message time ran out with a click.

He had an idea.

He let himself into the lab early, switched on a computer, wrote a message in an unbelievably small font. He printed, used a razor to cut around his message, which had become a dot. He used it to mark a butterfly.

When he was twenty-six, my father let a butterfly decide his destiny. He sat by the phone and waited. He sat and listened to her breathing.

One butterfly among millions fluttered among the clouds of orange wings headed for South America. It flew for weeks. It flew over towns, mountains, forests. It flew. Attached to its left wing was a tiny slip of paper. On the paper was a message so small that only a very careful person would notice it at all, let alone bother to place it under a microscope. But if they did, they would see it was squashed into a single word, the first word, the only one that ever meant anything anyway:

Iloveyou.

What can I say? My father believed in Fate.

Memory
The sun shines on the day of Danny's funeral. It feels wrong.

We enter in a group as usual, it seems horrible to go, but worse to stay away. Black mascara rivers course down Julia's cheeks; I guess she is the only one of us who really loved him.

Sun streams in the window and catches his hair, gives him a halo. They have combed his hair flat and I think I see a trace of make-up covering the darkness under his eyes. At least they haven't forced a smile on him. Maybe they couldn't.

His father stands alone in a corner looking hung-over, his mother flits about tearfully greeting relatives, neither look at their son's corpse, are they ashamed of him or themselves?

Perry stands by the head of the coffin. Danny's best friend – sidekick, really, but I don't think Perry ever minded. He is gentle, short but taller than me. He has freckles, sandy hair, is good at drawing and can't explain why he hates his name. As I watch, he takes a furtive look around him, slips a note in beside his friend's cold head, sidles away. Traffic rattles on the road outside.

We hover. We don't know what to say, how to act. Fifteen-year-olds aren't supposed to think about death.

I don't listen to the speeches. The priest didn't know him, Perry and Julia don't speak. The moment his parents turn to thank the priest, she throws a red rose into the pit. We look the other way.

I don't throw my handful of dirt on him. I don't want to help bury him.

There is a wake at a pub down the road. No one stops us from going in with the adults. Danny's mum stops acting the hostess. She quaffs her cheap sherry in one, lets out a single howl and begins to bawl helplessly. The little glass drops to the floor, shatters.

I notice Perry is missing, gently shift Julia to someone else's shoulder, walk back to the graveyard.

He is sitting on the grave of Ronald Murray and his beloved wife, Charlotte, R.I.P. Why don't they just write the whole thing?

'Hey.' He sniffs, looks up.

'Hey.' I sit down next to him. He plucks at the grass on the grave.

'Chaya, what d'you reckon happens after you die?'

'Dunno.'

'Me neither.' I want to comfort him, but as always I don't know what to say. He sighs and lies back on the grave. I lie back too. We look at the clouds. I apologise in my head to the Murrays.

'Chaya?'

'Yeah?'

'Why do we have to grow up?' I laugh a little; hope he thinks I have the most beautiful laugh in the whole wide world.

'I don't know, Perry.' I slip my cold hand into his. A tear runs from the corner of his eye. He squeezes my hand. We grow up.

It is never wise to put too much faith in a butterfly. One among millions once performed a miracle. But after the miracle? The veil was put away, the wedding flowers wilted. Marriage itself is not lace but something more practical, a patchwork quilt of habits, defining moments, clumsily stitched together, somehow made ... useful.

They flew back to England, bought a house with red window sills. He said Welcome Home. She planted sunflowers. He learned to cook pasta. He gambled at the pub on Friday nights, she stayed home, made lists for everything. He bought a stepladder, painted an orange butterfly on the ceiling above their bed. Years passed. She crept up behind him, planted a kiss on the back of his neck, nose buried in his black hair that smelled only of her. She gave birth almost painlessly, their dark-haired daughter fell asleep listening to his raspy 'Fields of Gold'.

They were happy...ish.

Thought

It is hard to write about ferrying into Venice at dusk without sounding corny.

What can I say? The stars are emerging, the water lapping, silhouette of the three-domed Cathedral in the distance, warm breeze, I'm half-expecting the moon to burst into song. The only others on this part of the deck are some young Italians. One snaps open a guitar case. Soon two couples are dancing, while the others perch daringly on the rail, clapping, singing badly. One catches my eye, winks. I smile back. (I can't wink, would I have dared to, anyway?)

I suddenly feel very alone, or out of my depth, or something. I pull my mother's coat tighter. Turning to go below deck, I find myself face to face with the winker. He smiles widely, his teeth criss-cross slightly, standing out white against rough olive skin. He speaks fast in Italian, I don't catch a word.

'*Scusa, Signore?*'

'*Ah, Inglese.*' He nods, grinning. '*Ballare, Signorina?*' Very slowly. *Ballare*...to dance.

'*No, grazie Signore...*' but he's laughing, he takes my hands, we spin across the deck, his friends are laughing, I'm laughing, his hands are warm, it's good to be alive.

The boy with the guitar starts a slower song, the sunlight fades, but the lights of Venice draw close. We turn slowly on the spot; I'm dancing with a complete stranger, why do

I feel safe? He looks down at me, takes a hand off my waist to point at himself, says, 'Santo.'

I point at myself. 'Chaya.'

'Chaya.' He tastes my name, laughs, '*Bellissima, Signorina* Chaya!'

A little later, I walk down a ramp in the dark, and I am in Venice. Santo asks me with his hands to go with him. I hesitate, but smile, shake my head. He seizes my shoulders, kisses both cheeks, wanders off into the night. I shrug off regret. Crossing the Ponte della Paglia, I pause in the middle, make a wish to return. With Perry.

I'm tired. I resolve to explore in the morning. The window above my bed in the hotel opens directly on to a narrow canal. Tomorrow I will see the Cathedral, the square full of pigeons, the bell tower, glass shops, flowers in window boxes, little bridges, but I could never love anything about Venice more than hearing that water lapping, later a gondola passing under my window sill.

At reception, I find a postcard has been waiting for me. From Perry, who doesn't believe in Fate. He has painted over the original picture...a butterfly. He's been talking to my mother.

Iloveyou.

In my room, I take out my notebook, sit on my window sill, feet dangling above the dark water.

It is never a good idea to fall in love with someone just because they're from somewhere you haven't been to. Or just because they can make you laugh even though they're speaking Italian, which you don't understand. Or because their hair smells of lemon blossom. And it is most definitely a mistake to fall in love with someone just because someone else once whispered to you that there is such a thing as Fate.

The thing about mistakes is that, idiotic as it is to make them in the first place, it would be a whole lot more idiotic when, a million years ago, your mother did the exact same thing.

What my mother never told my father was that she fell in love in Mexico.

The team was on its way back from South America, the miracle had been performed, but she didn't care. They stopped overnight in Mexico City. There was a party at someone's cousin's place, some of the group decided to go, dance, drink, they were young.

My mother is shy, and she only drinks medicinally. She found herself in the kitchen, cutting up lemons for people's drinks, which seemed unnecessary, it was just a party, but it gave her something to do. In that whitewashed kitchen, next to a large brown vase of sunflowers, my mother met the only person she would ever fall in love with. She told me this two weeks ago.

'What was he like then?' I asked.

'She.'

'*She?*'

'She.'

That explained a lot.

She was Italian. My mother never found out what she was doing in Mexico. It didn't matter. Her name was Volante. She also spoke Spanish, but no English, my mother also spoke French, but no Italian. She had a sleek black ponytail, an explosive laugh, narrow hips, a beauty spot on her temple. She missed a lemon, cut her finger. My mother is the sort of person who carries sticking plasters in her purse. They laughed in the kitchen, my mother felt happier than she had in a long, long time. And safe, probably. She had her first drink. Rum, I believe. They danced, knocked over the sunflowers, broke the vase. They left the party before it had properly begun. They found a bookshop, bought an Italian–English dictionary. Ten minutes later my mother had worked out how to ask 'What do you believe in?', or close enough. Volante flipped through the dictionary, pointed to 'Love'.

They went to a restaurant, ate something spicy my mother could not remember the name of, talked with their faces, their hands. At some point in the evening, the cross my mother wore began to feel oddly heavy. She slipped into the bathroom, tried to meet her own eyes in the mirror. She cried. She tried to break the chain, it was too strong. I didn't ask why she couldn't have just undone the clasp. She wet a strip of toilet paper, sponged away her make-up. She bribed one of the waiters to let her out through the kitchen, left without paying her half of the bill.

Volante got impatient, went to the bathroom. She found only a strip of toilet paper with smeared imprints of her would-be lover's face. She folded it carefully into her handbag, paid the bill, walked out the front door.

Meanwhile, my mother was sobbing and running through the dark streets. She didn't need to run. No one was chasing her. Finding a phone box, she tried to regain her breath. She dialled. It rang six and a half times before he picked up.

'Please marry me.'

What my father never told my mother was nothing.

Memory
Time does strange things in airports, but stranger things in hospitals. Here, people aren't waiting to fly from London to New York or London to Florence, but from the womb into

this life, from this life to the next. People are waiting to say the last, the only real goodbye. These gleaming corridors are washed not only with two kinds of tears, but with blood. In the emergency ward, a lifetime can take two seconds. In this waiting room, a night is an eternity.

We are waiting. Dad puts his arm around me. She asked him not to come in to the delivery room, even though fathers are supposed to.

My grandparents arrive. Gran's eyes are watering.

'He will have a Jewish name also, yes?' Grandad asks Dad.

'Paz,' I say. 'You once told me it was the most beautiful name.' I have never heard Gran laugh before, never seen her look so...alive. Grandad pats my hair.

'This girl, she is having a memory like the opposite of a sieve, no?'

We are waiting.

I sleep.

I wake.

I sleep...

Something is wrong.

A pale man in a blue cap is talking to Dad. Then he leads us to a room where my mother is sitting in bed, looking utterly blank, rocking, holding something small, so small, the wrong colour, not moving.

Dad tries to comfort her, she turns away from him. His face contorts, he turns, hits his head on the wall, hard, again and again.

Gran starts to sob. It sounds like a wounded animal crying.

Long ago, my grandparents sat in the sun, on the dry dirt, eating potatoes. They watched the children play. He smiled, told her: 'We are learning to live again.'

She drew a circle in the dust. 'I had a son.'

It was the first time he heard her speak. 'What was his name?'

'Paz.' She pulled her shawl tighter around her.

'That's the most beautiful name.'

'He was the most beautiful boy. Gold skin, gold hair, always laughing, they said I must've got him straight out of heaven...'

'I'm sorry.' He took her hand. She didn't feel it.

'Have this potato, I don't want...'

'Are you married?'

'No.'

'I'm sorry.'

The sun warmed their backs. He put his arm around her, brushed the hair from her wet face, kissed away a tear.

'It will be all right.'

Thought

'Don't stay in Rome,' they told me. 'It's crowded, it's smelly, it's expensive. Find yourself a nice little campground on the outskirts, go in for the day and do the whole tourist thing.' So here I am, clutching camera and phrasebook.

Buildings sag under heat and history.

Why now, I don't know, but suddenly the bad things are catching up with me. I can't run forever. I try not to think about them, I try not to think.

Colosseum...dry dust sticks to my sweaty legs. I squint, think I see faint red stains on the arena far below. This city has a long memory.

Sistine Chapel...I try to be overwhelmed. The most spectacular artwork. Such dedication to God. Did they really believe? I sit on a step, rest my head against a cool marble pillar. A loudspeaker constantly blares requests for respectful silence in various languages.

My shirt is sticking to my back. I pay too many euros for a strawberry *gelato.*

What am I doing here?

I realise I forgot to notice what it smells like in the Sistine Chapel. I may never return to this city in my life, but all I want is to be in the quiet campground with my notebook.

In the streets I carefully avoid rabid dogs and beggars' eyes.

I feel I'm suffocating. This isn't right. I skip dinner, take a taxi back out of the city. I'm avoiding the metro, it reminds me of London. I nearly wrote Home then, but London is not Home.

The campground is peaceful. I sit with my notebook outside the tent I rented. I watch the shadows stretch, some children playing, running between the trees. As the warm night thickens, fireflies appear from nowhere. The children chase them, shrieking happily. I've never seen fireflies before.

Before the nightmare, my grandmother lived in Warsaw. She married young. Her first husband was proud, a banker, and used to sing their son to sleep every night.

They had a son.

Gran loved Paz, her golden boy, more than herself, her husband, life. After her husband had sung him to sleep she would sneak in to wake him up for one last hug, one last kiss, she wanted hers to be the face in his dreams. She stole coins from the till at the shop where she worked to buy sweets for him, despite the rising costs of such luxuries. When he came home crying because of the pointing, chanting of 'Jew, smelly Jew', she was glad for the excuse to keep him home, cook for him, read to him, listen to him laugh all day. When she and her husband became unemployed, she starved herself to feed Paz, though the child always tried to slip the food back on to her plate.

Eventually, though they sold all their belongings, they could no longer afford the rent. They decided to walk through the city to Gran's sister's house, be safe, for a while. Gran insisted they all wear the armband with the blue and white star, despite her husband's protests.

In the middle of the city they passed an officer in a brown uniform. Gran pulled Paz close to her, bowed her head low. Her husband didn't look down quickly enough.

'Jews!' They stopped. Passers-by kept their distance as they hurried past.

'What are you doing on the footpath?' They stared, numb. Paz tugged on his mother's skirt.

'In the gutter!' My grandmother hurried her son off the footpath. Her husband stood, looking into the face of the other man, their eyes were level. The officer strode over to the gutter, put the barrel of his gun to Paz's forehead. My grandmother screamed, he hit her, she fell.

The officer looked around, smiling.

'Move, Jew.' Paz stood strangely still, watching his father. Why couldn't the man just walk in the gutter?

A shot. A spray of red. A boy lying in the street with no face. Blood in the gutter. Gran made a terrible noise crawled to her son's body rocked him in the gutter made a terrible noise didn't hear the second shot didn't see her husband crumple didn't care stopped believing.

I don't know why it had to happen. I don't know why the officer didn't kill her too; make a clean job of it. I don't know how long she sat in the pool of her son's blood.

I don't know who took the bodies from the street. I don't know how she survived the following years when she no longer cared whether she lived or died. I don't know.

Memory

When my father died, no one was sure if it was an accident or not. Later, my mother told the police: 'Of course it was an accident. My husband believed in Fate.'

Can anyone believe in anything completely?

It is the seventh anniversary of Paz's would-be birth. It rains bullets. My mother shuts herself in her room all day. My father goes to the pub.

Living a lie is much easier when you don't know it's a lie.

He doesn't come home.

I wait.

In the morning, I call the police.

They find his car wrapped around a thick tree trunk beside the road home. His friends from the pub don't recall that he drank much, just sat about lookin' bloody miserable, didn'e? But then, the road was wet.

The next weeks are darkness.

I sleep.

I wake.

I sleep...

The morning of the funeral, my mother puts make-up on me, I don't stop her. She braids my hair.

'Chaya, do you want to hear a story?'

'I'm too old, Mum.'

'Still.'

She tells me about Mexico. Volante. How many times she's thought of going to Italy.

'Do you even know the woman's surname?'

'I didn't mean I'd go to look for her, as such.'

'Do you believe in Fate?'

She purses her lips. 'Sometimes.'

'Mum?'

'What, Chaya?'

'Do you love Dad?'

She pulls the chain at the back of her neck. 'You mean "*Did* you love Dad?"'

I don't go to my father's funeral.

I wipe off the make-up. I cut off my braid. Our house fills with the smell of burning hair. I turn on the TV because I can't stand the silence. I look through my parents' chest of drawers. I find a drawer of lists.

Happiness of stories
Sadness of the inescapable story
Happiness of a sea so wide
Sadness of a sea so deep
Happiness of being loved
Sadness of loving
Happiness of maps
Sadness of a world too big, or too small
Happiness of lies
Sadness of knowing you know they're lies
Happiness of graveyards (lives, loves, lost, but they were here)
Sadness of long-wilted flowers
Happiness of sunlight on eyelids
Sadness of knowing the sun is dying, and the eyelids
Happiness of tears
Sadness of waterproof mascara

I find a drawer of lottery tickets. I take it out, I count them. He even kept them in order. For the first few years after he was old enough to buy them, he's used my mother's birth date and age in various combinations. Later, my birth date. Then Paz's. The last ticket is the day he died.

What am I doing here?

I look up a travel agent in the Yellow Pages. I empty my bank account, my inheritance. I pack minimal clothes, my mother's coat, my passport, shampoo, toothbrush, notebook. I don't speak to my mother for several days, then when I'm ready I leave her a note, a list of hotel addresses I know she won't read. I take a taxi to Heathrow.

From the airport I call Perry, get the answerphone, can't think of anything to say.

Too many thoughts

Language is a clumsy thing. Why can't our thoughts just sublime? From pure meaning into gaseous human feeling, to be inhaled by one and all? Why must we label things, always label? The label becomes the thing; any real meaning gets bored and wanders off. Labels are too clear-cut, why does the line between fact and fiction have to be so sharp? Perilously sharp. Anything that falls on the divide is killed, and its corpse becomes invisible. Yet languages, labels, are all we have.

I'm sitting watching children, fireflies, flicking through my notebook. My father believed in Fate, my mother tries to believe in God, my grandparents believe in everything and nothing, what do I believe? What is it I've been trying to say?

I will spend my life trying to bridge the gap between meaning and feeling, fact and fiction, make the passage pure, reach the unreachable truth. True artists tickle it almost by accident with their brushes, writers' hands touch its surface but leave it stained with ink, so all we get is light through a dirty window.

Musicians find only a small range of notes can be heard, artists find there are only so many possible colours, and no paint contains light, we are all bound by the limits of words, but we try.

We are all chasing fireflies, our beliefs, some sort of meaning; those who don't chase don't live. So we chase. Not to catch it, suffocate it with our hands, but just to get close enough to see its light on our fingertips. Even with a million miles of darkness ahead, to see one light in the distance is enough. To see its light in the eyes of another wanderer, to feel its warmth between you and call it love, is enough. To wonder at the chance of the occasional touching of souls, is it chance? Is there such a thing as Fate? It doesn't matter.

We are here, this is real, this matters. It is enough to keep me going. To keep the whole wide world turning. To keep us alive.

MAIKI

KINGI McKINNON

Right from the very day he was born, there was something different about Maiki. Just what, I couldn't really say. It wasn't anything you could put a finger on – it was just something...*felt*...*sensed*. I was the only one who noticed. Somehow, something just didn't feel right.

Sure, he had a dimple that the others didn't have, but *that* was the only subtle difference. He had the same hair, skin and hazel eyes, but what alerted me seemed to come from *within*. Like he had an aura. Yes, an actual physical presence that only I seemed to pick up on. I'd never felt anything like that before – not in my entire life, so naturally it puzzled me a little. It was like a premonition. A sort of *foreboding* of things to come.

He was squinting, trying to size me up I'm sure, the day I took him and Raukura home from the hospital. I looked down into his tiny screwed-up face, and I can swear he stared discerningly back – like a little wise old man. Although Raukura said he couldn't properly focus yet, I was pretty certain he could. It was a weird feeling.

'He's such a good baby,' she enthused when we got home and she fed him from her breast. 'He sleeps all night and doesn't make a peep.'

'Well that's a good start,' I assured her as I hovered over them both.

When milking time came round, I was reluctant to leave, but some things have to be done. We run a little farm, you see. Only thirty acres, with a small herd of cows, chickens, two horses, half a dozen pigs at most times, and a few head of hogget for Sunday roasts.

It doesn't pay a great fortune, but it gives us a roof over our heads, feeds the whanau, and keeps the kehua from the door.

Maiki grew up fast. You had to around our neck of the woods, or you dipped out badly. By the age of four, he was already proving competitive in most things, matching his two brothers and sister in speed, wit and dexterity.

He displayed skills and talents that, for his age, were outstanding. He was intelligent, creative, naturally athletic, and he had a charisma and charm that drew people and animals to him like a magnet. I was intrigued, *awed*, watching these abilities grow with him; secretly and proudly from a distance.

What made him tick? Did he possess some supernatural power, and if so – why?

He took to school like a duck to water, gaining good grades and popularity in a very short time. Pere, Tuku and our daughter, Marama, did well too, but in time, most of the awards, miniatures and certificates festooning the walls, shelves and refrigerator belonged to him.

Everything came easily and naturally. The dedication, effort and commitment required to excel never seemed to apply to him. He was fearless as well, which made me a little apprehensive at times.

I'd taught them all to ride and swim at an early age, but he was happy only when at full gallop, or swimming in the deepest, most dangerous parts of the river. Often I'd take time to talk to him, to explain why he shouldn't do these things that scared the life out of his mother. He listened dutifully, but it only went in one ear and out the other. When I think of it now, it was like he was trying to live his life at a fast pace and gain all the thrills he could before he ran out of time.

'Don't let that dog lick your face,' I warned him one day. 'He'll give you hydatids.'

'What's hydatids?' he queried.

It was still early days – the disease was practically unheard of. Hospitals knew of it, but as yet there hadn't been any outbreak. Nevertheless, sheep owners were being instructed to bury their dead animals rather than leave them exposed; but no one was really listening.

'Sheep measles,' I told him. 'Bugs that get in your guts and eat out your organs, I hear. If dogs have been eating dead sheep, they can pass the disease on to you. Or if you chew grass like I've seen you do sometimes, you can get it from there. Where the sheep have been.'

He pulled a face then, and shoved the dog away. 'Yuk, I think he already has been,' he said, rubbing at his face with the back of his jersey sleeve. 'He's been over to Bailey's, and his breath smells like rotten sheep.'

'Well give your face a darned good scrub and keep him right away from you,' I warned. 'Don't think it'll be very pleasant having bugs munching you out from the inside.'

Maiki loved farm life. He thrived on the many joys and pleasures it brought each day. Even at only eleven years of age, he realised that to enjoy the fruits of life, one had to do the hard yards, and he did so without a moan. He knew watermelon and sweet corn, his favourites, didn't just pop up out of the ground. Someone had to plant the seed.

He helped with all the other chores too, without having to be told; unlike his older brothers who did so only when they had to and lived solely for the day they could escape to the city. Marama had the same attitude. Her mother always had to drive her.

I tried hard not to show favouritism, but it was pretty difficult. There was something between me and Maiki. A rapport. Of all my kids, he was the one most like me, and I don't just mean in ability or his finer points. I mean in the way he thought and felt about things. We were on the same sort of wavelength, and enjoyed each other's company.

If we went out eeling, it was him who carried on further upstream with me, long after the others had quit. If a job required working on into the darkness, again, it was him who stuck it out with me. He brought a lot of pleasure into my life, Maiki.

★

It was at the end of his first year in high school that things took a change for the worse in our household. Maiki, as expected, had achieved greatly, taking his first noteworthy steps into academia, and demonstrating his physical skills in a more significant sports arena.

I remember clearly the day he came home from the orchard up in the bush, bent almost double, and clutching his stomach – complaining of a stitch-like pain that wouldn't go away.

Marama was close behind, looking concerned, as was their cousin, Hariata, who was there for the summer holidays.

Later, when he was in his room resting, I asked them for a detailed account.

'He fell out of the apricot tree,' Marama said simply. 'There was only one apricot on it, and it looked fat, juicy and ripe. He climbed right to the top of the tree to get it, the branch broke, and he landed flat on his back. We thought he was only winded.'

Later, just before milking time, I went in to see how he was faring, and he said it still hurt.

'Well climb right into bed,' I told him, '... and stay there. Have a good rest, and I'll drop in and see you when I get back from milking.'

I frowned, concerned, as he struggled into his pyjamas, then flopped into bed. It was dark and he was fast asleep when Pere went in to get him at teatime.

'You have to eat something,' his mother urged, as he pushed the food around on his plate. She'd outdone herself, having cooked and stuffed one of the fowls and a cockerel and served them up with fresh beans, carrots and new potatoes from the garden. Maiki, like all of us, adored her stuffing and new potatoes.

'There's a rhubarb pie for dessert after,' she coaxed, 'and Dad brought home some cream.'

'Not hungry' is all he muttered, before excusing himself and going back to bed.

He wasn't hungry the next morning either, or the next; and the pain was still there.

It was almost a week later that we decided we'd better take him in to see the doctor. We'd both hoped he'd gradually snap out of it, but as it turned out, he hadn't. Already, he looked gaunt and sallow, having eaten nothing, and, I suspected, he hadn't been sleeping either.

No matter what time of the day or night I went in to check, he'd just be lying there, staring forlornly at the ceiling. His tray, when it returned from his bedroom, was still the same as it was when it went in, with not a morsel disturbed or missing. Food, it seemed, was the last thing on his mind.

'I'm afraid you're going to have to take him to the hospital for further tests,' Doctor Corbett told us after she'd examined him. 'I'm not sure what it is, but there's something definitely wrong inside. Something could have burst, or got badly bruised. I don't know. They'll have to run more tests and give him an X-ray.'

The word *hospital* worried him, and I didn't blame him. It worries us all. However, if you want to get better, then it's the best place to be.

'Hydatids,' the house surgeon told us after a lengthy examination. 'My god, the very first case in the country. We're going to have to admit him.'

Maiki cried when we broke the news to him. Just softly to himself, and I must admit, I shed a tear or two myself. He cried, not because he had hydatids or anything else related to the disease, but because he wasn't going home with us again. He'd never been apart from us in his life. Me, I cried for the unknown. Just the fact that he was being admitted was enough. I'd seen too many people I'd loved go in there, and come out in a box.

His treatment for the first week or two was pretty hectic. Blood tests, X-rays and every other type of test you can imagine. Though we'd like to have visited every day, sometimes it was downright impossible. It was a good forty miles to the hospital – a long way to travel daily, and we had other important commitments.

Maiki understood though, and never once complained, just being happy to see us when we could make it. He was beginning to resemble a pincushion from all the needles they'd been poking into him.

It was about three weeks later when we noticed they had stepped up his treatment. We walked into his room one afternoon and there he was, lying in his bed with a tube protruding from his stomach. I gasped when I saw the size of the needle. It was almost the same width as a pencil, but longer so it could penetrate deep.

On the floor was a bucket, and grinning, Maiki summoned me to have a look.

'Pea soup,' he grinned. 'You want some pea soup, Dad?'

I peered into the half-filled bucket, awestricken and silent. It really did look like pea soup. It was thick and green and flowed steadily from within. The narrow hose had a small tap halfway along.

'Be back in a moment,' I told them, and I set off to find the doctor. Doctor Gibson was very co-operative.

'It's a build-up,' she told me. 'The disease is in his stomach.

He's not in any pain,' she assured me, 'we gave him an anaesthetic to numb him. His stomach was very swollen.'

'Also,' she told me, 'he's going to require an operation, but it's not up to me to tell you when. Only the surgeon will know when he's examined him further. We'll get in touch with you then, and you'll have to sign some consent forms.'

Later, back in his room, it was difficult to keep the smile on my face. He looked so thin and pallid, his cheeks gaunt and sunken, and he'd lost lots of weight. I tried hard not to think of tupapaku – dead bodies – when I looked at him.

Raukura and I were there when it came time for his operation. We took Marama with us because she insisted on coming. We sent the boys to my sister, Hiko.

He wasn't quite with us when we arrived at the hospital. They'd given him a needle to calm and soothe him just before we arrived.

His face was deathly pale, and his arms and legs were like pipe cleaners. I closed my eyes and uttered a silent karakia. Begged our atua to look after him and return him safely.

He waved, grinning foolishly from the trolley when it arrived to take him to the theatre, and we waited. For two and a half hours solid we waited, till they wheeled him back into the ward. He was still heavily sedated, but the operation had gone successfully, the sister assured us. Apparently his stomach had been full of cysts and daughter cysts. He wouldn't awaken for a while though, as he was in an induced coma. He wouldn't be coherent until the following day.

His pyjama top was unbuttoned, and I felt sick inside when I saw the thick bandages held in place with rolls of sticking plaster. There were green spreading stains all over them, and I wished it had been me who had been afflicted. I would gladly have borne the pain and suffering for him.

'He has a few drains,' she told us, 'to drain off the excess fluid.'

The next day when we went back he was in a lot of pain. The anaesthetic had worn off, the stitches pulled every time he moved, and they changed the bandages three times a day.

'It hurts,' he said, 'because they stick to the stitches and drains and pull at them. And the smell.' He pulled a face. 'All the gunk coming out is like pus. It drenches my pyjamas and the sheets. Sometimes I'm lying in a big puddle.'

I couldn't say anything. Neither could his mother. All we could do was hug him as tightly as we dared and assure him everything was for the best.

'Taihoa, e tama,' I encouraged. 'Just wait. You're on the road to recovery now.'

But he wasn't. He caught an H-bug from scratching the raw wound with his dirty fingers when it started itching during the healing process, and the wound had become infected and burst open. There was pus coming from that area now, the sister told us before we went into the ward, and it was all the surgeon could do to close it.

Maiki was still crying when we went in. His face was turned to the wall and he sobbed brokenly into his pillow. I had never felt so helpless in my life.

'I…I'm sorry, my son,' I whispered, wanting him to know I shared his pain. It tore at my very soul to see him in such agony and there was nothing I could do about it.

'It…it really hurt,' he said between sobs when he could finally talk again. 'The…doctor just squeezed the edges of the operation together with his bare hands and…and held it, while the nurse put strips of plaster across to keep it in place.'

At home, I barely slept that night, and when we went back next day, we found him crying again. Now he wasn't generally a cry-baby, Maiki. He hated like hell for anyone to see him weep. At home I always knew I'd find him in the woodshed when he was upset about something, but here, there wasn't anywhere to hide.

This time he showed me his thigh. It astounded me that his legs had become even thinner, and when I saw the swelling and bruising, I stomped off to find some answers.

The needle, he told us, was thicker than the others, and they applied it like throwing a dart into a board. Then they had to administer its contents very slowly to avoid it bubbling out, and it burnt every millimetre of the way. He had to endure it first thing in the morning, and last thing at night, and the sound of the treatment trolley rattling closer and closer to his bed each time was like something from a horror story.

'I know it's painful, but it's totally necessary, Mr Manu,' the sister told me. 'He's a very brave boy and we're doing our best. At the moment, we need to give him penicillin morning and night to clear up the infections. Also, we're dosing him with morphine to try and keep the pain down to a minimum.'

Then, just as we felt he was finally getting better, they found the horrible disease had manifested in his right lung. It seemed like we were all being punished for something we hadn't done.

How much more can such a puny body take? I thought a couple of weeks later when they returned him from the theatre for the second time.

The surgeon and two of his trainees were still around his

bed, checking that the drips were in place, when they allowed us into his room. He looked very concerned and caring.

'How are you, Mr and Mrs Manu?' He nodded politely when he saw us. 'I think we might have got it all this time. He was very badly affected, and I'm afraid we've had to remove half of his right lung this time. He's a brave lad. You should be proud of him...'

I don't know how long I sat there after they'd left, just stroking his hair and feeling close to him. 'Why the hell does it have to happen to him?' I snorted bitterly. 'There's people out there who commit crimes and hurt people every day, and they're never punished for it. This fulla's done nothing to anyone. Why the hell does He have to pick on him?'

'Shhh, dear. Don't blame *Him*. Let's just be grateful we still have our son,' Raukura said, squeezing my hand. 'We could have lost him a couple of times.'

This time they kept him in an induced coma for a week, and when we went in to see him at the end of that time, he was sitting up in bed, smiling. The colour too seemed to be actually returning to his face, and as usual he was delighted to see us.

'I was awake during the operation,' he told us excitedly. 'I remember everything.'

'Aww, you must have been dreaming, boy,' I teased. 'They wouldn't keep you awake during such a serious oper-ation as that.'

'They did, Dad,' he insisted. 'He said I was too skinny and weak to anaesthetise.'

'But what about the pain?' I asked. 'They removed part of your lung, man.'

'I know,' he grinned. 'They cut out parts of my ribs too,

so they could get to it. I'll tell you what he did. There was only me...him...and the nurse, right? Well they gave me what he called a lumbar puncture. It's a needle in the spine, see, and it numbs everything, the nurse told me. You don't feel a thing. I didn't either.'

I was amazed he could remember such a term, but he'd picked up quite a few medical terms since he'd been in there.

'The nurse was holding on to me,' he continued. 'I was leaning over her shoulder. Man, it was spooky. I even heard the bones crack when he cut my ribs. The poor nurse, though, must have really been getting tired, cos I was in the same position all the way through the operation. Towards the end I remember laughing and talking, and my voice was echoing all around the theatre, and I could see myself looking down from the ceiling. Then suddenly I was on the trolley being taken back to the ward.'

That worried me a bit. He'd had an out–of–body experience by the sound of it, and it could have been a telling moment. I fought hard to keep my emotions in check. I wanted to cry. To offer karakia and thanks, all at the same time, but for our boy's sake, I kept myself in check.

'I've got a big drain sticking out of the back of my chest too.' He frowned. 'It's different to the others. It's like a small hose, and it's got a big thing like a ball inside with a hole in it so the gunk can run out. It's got a plug in the end too. A spiggot that they pull out so the stuff can drain into a bowl.'

'Well that's got to be good,' I assured him quietly. 'At least it's getting rid of it.'

'Yeah, I guess,' he said doubtfully. 'I'm just thinking about when they pull it out though. It's only got a little hole to come out of.'

★

Six weeks later, it exited with barely a pop, and our son was finally allowed home. He'd grown a lot, both physically and mentally, and for some reason I felt awkward around him. Like he was a stranger, not our son. We'd celebrated his thirteenth birthday in there a couple of weeks before, but I guess that was no reason to feel the way I did.

It was good having him home. Good to see him eating again. He could really wolf down a good feed. He'd changed though, somewhat. We'd all noticed after he'd been home a while. He wasn't quite the same caring, friendly boy he was before he'd gone into hospital. He'd become a little cocky, or arrogant, for want of a better word. He strutted a bit and had developed a sarcastic, caustic wit.

A few times he had run-ins with his older brothers, and I almost had to pull them apart. He delighted in baiting his sister too, and sometimes reduced her to tears.

'Just be patient,' I pleaded with them when I got them alone. 'He's had that horrible disease, and it will take him a while to readapt.'

But instead of getting better, things got worse. He even started back-chatting his mother, and pushing his luck with me. I didn't really know how to handle it. I tried reasoning with him, trying to point out how he was upsetting the household and how we all just wanted him better so he could move on. But each time I looked at him, all I could see was a pathetic little boy with drips in his skinny arms, and the horrible scars left from the operations. My heart bled for him.

The one that had burst open looked like a huge ugly spider. The scars the drains had left, and the hole where the bits of ribs had been removed, would always draw pitying looks.

How would a young man react to that on the sports field, eh? Not that I felt he would ever get back there. How would it look to a sweetheart when the time came?

All I could do was sigh and feel sad for him, knowing his life from here on would be a hard row to hoe.

He wasn't happy going back to school, but I hoped that would change when he settled back in. That he'd become the achiever he was before his illness. But it wasn't to happen. He started hassling teachers and disrupting classes, almost to the stage where they just didn't want him there any more. Also, he'd got in with the bad element, and although our town was only tiny, they soon found places where they could wag school. How could he have been the same boy who'd left home less than a year ago?

The day he'd come home late and obviously half drunk was almost the last straw. The headmaster had brought him back just on dusk, and for the first time in my life I came close to hitting one of my kids with a closed fist.

'What the hell's the matter with you, mate?' I pleaded after the headmaster had gone. 'You've never done anything this stupid before. You're hurting us, boy – me and your mother. We *all* love you, e hoa, but your crazy antics . . . they're tearing this family apart.'

What hurts me now when I think of it was he seemed completely comfortable with it, patting me on the back and grinning a crazy lopsided grin.

'S'all right, Dad,' he kept trying to reassure me. 'I feel good . . . I really do.'

He tried to hug me, and I snapped. All those months of caring – worrying ourselves until we were almost as sick as he was – and now these shenanigans were almost the last straw.

'*It's not just about you any more,*' I suddenly snapped,

grabbing his shirtfront and instinctively shoving him back to punching distance. *'It's about all of us.'*

My voice broke on a near-hysterical sob as all the worries and frustrations of the past year came bubbling to the surface. My hand balled into a fist and I was about to let fly when Raukura appeared out of nowhere and dragged down on my arm.

'Don't you dare hit that boy,' she snarled coldly. 'What sort of man would hit a kid with his fist when he's in this state, eh? Especially one as sick as he's been. You should feel very ashamed of yourself, Arapeta Manu.'

'Come on, e kare,' she said gently, wrapping a protective arm around our son and leading him away. 'You climb into the bath then come and get some tea.'

After, I did feel ashamed of myself. Totally. How could I have even contemplated hitting him? Head bowed, I mooched on down to the tractor shed and sat slumped there for hours, watching the crescent moon creep across the velvet sky and wondering how things had got so bad, before the icy fingers of a fast-approaching winter finally drove me home.

The kids were all in bed when I arrived back. Raukura came to me and hugged me without saying a word. Rested her head on my chest and silently accepted the unspoken apology that dripped from my cheeks into her hair.

Maiki did get suspended eventually. He wasn't expelled.

It was nothing personal, the headmaster assured me, and I believed him, knowing he'd genuinely tried to help. Ranginui Wilson and I went back a long way. Had grown up together and were whanaunga.

'It's the Board's decision,' he assured me. 'He needs time

out to get things back into perspective. When he's done that, we'll be glad to take him back, Albie.'

He looked thoughtful, knowing how bad I was hurting.

'You know,' he added as an afterthought, 'the one or two other times he arrived back at school drunk to catch the bus home, he seemed completely different. Kind of... mellow. Y'know what I mean? Co-operative. Might be something to think about. Anyway, it's a damn shame it had to happen. He's got plenty of potential, that boy.'

At home, he was very restless. For the first week or two he tried hard to concentrate on schoolwork, but found it impossible. Most of the time he was short-tempered and moody, and snapped at everyone and everything.

They were side effects, Doctor Corbett told me when I approached her to see if she could help. What he'd undergone was very traumatic, and a change in his behaviour was to be expected. He'd come right eventually.

Other times he rode the horses, or lost himself up the river with an eeling spear. Before long there were dried eels all over the fence and clothesline, and we were giving them away to the rellies and neighbours as fast as he brought them in.

Then he started roaming the hills and bush. Raukura and I accepted it all in silence. Tried to be compliant and flexible as long as his actions didn't affect anyone else. We no longer drove him to do anything. 'He'll come around in his own time,' Doctor Corbett had advised.

Then one afternoon he came home happy and smiling, in a totally different mood to the one he'd left in. For a moment he resembled the Maiki of old, and my heart gave a lurch. Had some miracle happened?

But although he grinned a lot, and amused himself with Marama's kitten, there was something about him I couldn't quite put my finger on. It was his eyes – I know that now. They looked sort of vacant. Glassy.

Later, after he'd grabbed a bite and fooled about with his schoolbooks, he disappeared again, and we didn't see him until teatime. After that it became a sort of ritual where he'd eat breakfast, then disappear again till lunch. Sometimes he didn't arrive home until tea. And all the time he'd be in that weird, detached mood.

'He smells funny,' I heard Marama whisper to Pere one night.

'Yeah,' Pere frowned. 'Like ... like shoe polish ... or kerosene or something, eh. He acts weird too. Laughs at nothing.'

They both giggled.

I found out where he'd been going a few days later. I was down at the tractor shed, about to start the tractor up, when I heard him in the little room at the back, talking and laughing. It was where I kept the forty-four-gallon drum of petrol, and oil for the tractor and chainsaws. I wondered who he was in there with.

As the door swung open I gasped aloud. 'Oh jeezus, boy, what the hell are you doing?'

The lid was off the petrol drum, his nose shoved deep into the hole, and he was breathing in the fumes.

I dragged him roughly away and he stumbled, almost tripping. He was miles away, his eyes vacant and out of it, as though he was on another planet.

'*Are you trying to kill yourself?*' I all but screamed, shaking him. 'Holy Christ, man, you almost died in that bloody hospital, and now you're trying to finish the job off. Come on,' I growled, grabbing him by the collar of his shirt, and shoving him homeward. 'You're coming home, and you better bloody well stay there.'

He was sullen and defiant by the time we got there. The effect the fumes had on him had all but worn off. I sat him down at the kitchen table and told Raukura what he'd been up to. She went around and hugged him to her breast.

'Oh my boy,' she sighed forlornly, rocking him. 'What are you doing to yourself, eh? What are you doing, tamaiti?'

Later, after I'd stopped shaking, I moved my chair a little closer and painfully reached for him. I wanted to hold him, comfort him, tell him we were there for him and always would be.

But he drew back instinctively, flinching and sucking in a frightened breath as he eyed me suspiciously, and I knew in that moment he'd never let me close again.

'Why, e tama?' I pleaded softly. 'Why are you doing this? Don't you know that stuff will kill you?'

He said nothing, just turned to his mother and buried his face against her. She took his hand and slid in on the form beside him, rubbing it reassuringly. 'It's true,' she said softly. 'Why, son? Where did you pick that up from?'

It was a long while before he said anything. 'Harry,' he said at last. His eyes were downcast and his voice sounded little more than a croak. 'Harry Witana and…and Zane Pouwhare.'

I knew who he meant. They were the boys he used to wag school with.

'But what's wrong with it?' he pleaded, looking puzzled. 'It just relaxes me – makes me feel good. And…and I see things – hear things, like at the movies. There's stuff going on all around and I see fairies and angels. I hear the birds calling out to me, and the trees and animals talking. It doesn't hurt anybody.'

I hung my head and shook it dazedly. 'Oh my god, it

does, son,' I cried, desperately. 'It's hurting *you, can't* you understand? It's killing you slowly every time you stick your nose into that bloody drum. You're hallucinating cos it's loaded with chemicals and lead and god knows what other damaging stuff. It kills your brain cells and eats at your lungs. And you've already lost half of one. I know, son. Your mum's brother, Uncle Joey, is in the mental hospital because he used to do it too. It fried his brains.'

I gave up and looked pleadingly at Raukura – dear sweet Raukura, mainstay of our family – and begged silently that she say something that would convince him. Although her eyes were moist, she was staying strong, determined not to cry and show weakness. Our son needed urgent help, and blubbering like a big baby wasn't going to help anyone.

But it was too late to help him. We begged, threatened, even tried to keep him prisoner, but we couldn't watch him all the time. I put a big sturdy lock on the petrol shed and bought a locking cap for the tractor, but there were always plenty of other sources. Places I never thought to look.

He'd taken to syphoning it out of the car, and hiding it in cans and flagons along the river and up in the bush. Sometimes I found jars that bore traces, and I watched and followed, but it never stopped him.

Then one morning a few months later, he wasn't in his bed. We all looked for him. Hunted high and low, and I found him mid-morning, slumped across the motor mower out in the tool shed. He was stiff and cold, and the petrol cap from the mower was lying beside him. I didn't want the others to see him.

I closed the door, pushing a screwdriver into the jamb behind me and jamming it, then emptied some junk out of a box and sat down on it. His eyes were open and staring blankly, and there was a black oily smudge beneath his nostrils.

I didn't cry. I just suddenly felt drained and empty. Why? Why was he put here on this earth in the first place? It just seemed such a waste of time.

Later, I told Raukura and asked that she carry on being strong for the children till we'd sorted it out. She told them he'd been found and took them off somewhere to explain while I phoned the police and ambulance.

The tangi was quite large – he was well remembered. All his family and whanaunga came, and so did most of the pupils from his school. When they sang 'Whakaria Mai' I still felt blank. Empty. Nothing really made any sense. Maybe it does now.

All this happened a very long time ago. I'm old now, and my kids and their kids live in the city. Maiki, like his mother who joined him a few years ago, still lives on in my heart.

As always, everyone had answers after. It's the same old story. The barn door always closes after the horse has bolted.

It was the constant dosage of morphine that caused Maiki's addiction to petrol, the analysts reckoned. Maybe they're right. Like morphine or alcohol at a certain level, it had a calming effect, and he believed he was functioning better. Keeping calm and cool, if not collected.

I like to think my own theories are pretty accurate too. That the vibes I'd felt in the beginning *were* telling a story. That Maiki *was* different, and was only here on loan. His potential was a sign. An indication of the man he might have been, had he been allowed to stay. I don't know. It's all so complicated, and I still think it was a waste of time.

It took a long time to get over it. For a fulla who'd only stayed a short time, he'd made a big impact. How *could* I forget him? He'd been a part of me, part of my life.

'You need to get it out of your system,' Raukura told me almost a year later. She always knew. 'You need to have a good tangi and cleanse yourself so you can move on.'

She was right of course, and the opportunity came not long after. I was out riding one day, up along the river checking the yearlings, when sunlight suddenly reflected off something bright. On riding over to check, I found a glass jar. A jar, half-buried in the mud, with an oily residue around the bottom. I got slowly down from the horse, slumped to my knees, and bawled like a baby. How long I stayed there, I don't know, but after, as Raukura predicted, I felt better. And when I went home, she knew.

Yes, I don't know how, but somehow, Raukura always knew.

LUNG

HENRY FELTHAM

'Is he staring at me?'

    'He's not.'

    'You missed it.'

    'Leave him alone.'

    'He's sizing us up,' my brother hissed.

    'He's not even facing this way.'

    'That's what he *wants* you to think.'

    'Just eat your duck.'

We'd come this far down the Bund because I knew a place that did a good soup-in-winter-melon, but Jean-Yves had barely touched his. He looked away from the old *Chinois*, who was standing underneath a plane tree, and picked at his noodles with a perished plastic fork, letting them fall back into the soup. Drops of yellow flecked his shorts. He considered the mess.

'They put some strange stuff in this...' he searched for a word, settling on the English '...*shit*.'

'So you've said.' But I couldn't hear it again. What good would it do? I was bored with this paranoia of his, with this too-laden scene, the Custom House leering over us, card sellers hocking cheap off-colour portraits and key rings near the river-edge, the ever-shifting motion of it all gathered in the air, stirred but never shifted by a breeze off the slick Huangpu.

The old man gazed at the slow grizzle of cars up the roadway, cycle-taxis touting for fares among the tired shuffle of suits home, the buses' squeal of raw brakes. He hadn't noticed us squatting like bored sailors above the river's edge, but Jean-Yves watched him regardless.

'Jean!' I spat. 'Forget him. He doesn't give a fig about us!'

Jean turned towards me, looking around as though we might actually be being spied on. 'How do you know?' he whispered. 'Yesterday, I saw a woman lugging her brat along behind her, dragging his heels, and you know what she shouted at him?'

Whether I said anything or not, he was going to tell me.

'*Hurry up or I'll bite a piece out of you!*'

'So what.'

Jean's eyes opened wide, astonished at my obtuseness. 'If she hadn't noticed me, that kid would have been *finished*.'

I stared at the greasy halo of yolk-coloured soup caught in the edge of my pottle, evidence of a meal I hadn't really noticed eating. I stood, grabbed Jean-Yves's dinner – 'Hey!

What you...?' – and took them both to the bin.

When I came back I stood over him, gazing down. A clump of blonde hair had fallen over one eye, but the expression on his narrow face was familiar – lips pursed in a mirthless conspiracy of one, he had the insolent calm of a horse. Maybe I was worried over nothing.

'You nag me *all day* about coming down here, then don't even...' the corner of his mouth tilted slightly down and his face seemed to change entirely. I knew this expression too, but not on him. It was mine. He was mimicking the uncertainty on my face.

For a long moment he sat there.

'Let's go,' I said. Jean glanced at the bin, then at the old man. I heard myself sigh, 'Let's get out of here.'

'Okay,' he said, still staring.

'Come on.'

My brother stood up. I pushed him on and we started the long walk up the river home.

I sat by the window eating a croissant, watching the water stream off the roof in dirty runnels on to the street below. I was thinking about my brother and the rain; about both of them, neither. It can rain for days in August.

The street was nearly empty, cast in pale greys. A few people passed by, most of them under the balcony across the way, pressed against storefronts as the rain came licking in under the high roof. It was lunchtime and Jean-Yves still hadn't emerged from his room, but that was no great surprise. I'd done nothing, spent the morning reading then half an hour trying to write a letter, but abandoned it for sounding too bleak. Afterwards I went to his door, knocked and knocked again, a distant reply the third time.

'What?'

'You all right?'

'...fine...' As though he was out on the roof.

'You getting up?'

'...'

'What?' I shouted. 'D'you want breakfast? Some *lunch*?'

'...tired...fine...'

I went back to the letter, tried to find something of Shanghai's allure to recount, but no matter what I wrote it turned into a complaint. I should have rung someone, like the Monsieur encouraged us to, but I couldn't face a telephone call. I hate telephones, really. Eventually I gave up for a second time, scrunched the note into a ball and heaved it out the window. Guilt rose up like a spring tide, then fell away — who'd notice a scrap of paper in Shanghai? I went into the living room.

The furniture is imitation, but people never guess. There's a bookshelf, some scrolls and an unremarkable view of rooftops. You can just see the Mansions' deco crest in the distance, the city beyond it, though even if the rain hadn't obscured it today, the small woman crouched at the window would have.

Compact and delicate, with a tight bun of thin grey hair tied up with a *gung*, Mrs Su didn't hear me come in. I stood watching as she laid down a pair of scissors on the sill, then cast something into the air, where a sudden breeze blew it back into the room. She leaped up to catch it, surprisingly spry, and twisted to land facing me as the piece of paper fluttered to the ground between us.

'*Ni hao ma*, Mrs Su?'

Her eyes latched to the floor, but she muttered, '*Bien, et toi*?' in her clumsy, nasal French.

'*Bien*,' I answered, gazing at the figure on the floor. The poverty of my Chinese is almost total, but this was familiar, like someone almost smiling. 'It's beautiful,' I said, picking it up. The way children cut out snowflakes, she'd cut this from heavy paper. She looked like a chastened schoolgirl – tiny, presenting the crown of her head to me as she gazed at the floor. I handed the figure back to her and she grabbed it, crushing it in her haste. She stood that way, hands mashed together, then raised her eyes slightly.

'Clean room?'

I shook my head. We'd never had a maid in Tousec. Having a servant struck me as primitive and about as comfortable as wearing a loincloth. Regardless, I hadn't had time to mess the place up; the Monsieur was never here, and my brother never left his own room long enough to dirty another.

'Jean-Yves room?'

I laughed and her face fell to the carpet again.

'Is scenty,' she mumbled, and for maybe ten seconds more we stood like that. Finally she looked up, actually peered at me, then moved close until I could smell peanut oil on her breath. 'He sick?' she asked quietly, and I wasn't sure what to say, or if I even knew the answer. Then I saw the shape of it.

'Yes. A little sick.'

'Unbalance, *non*?'

My head nodded itself without any intention on my part.

'Need doctor?'

My jaw clamped shut and I felt myself blink heavily. 'No. I don't think a doctor would help.'

'Know good doctor,' she whispered, her warm breath floating over my face. 'No medical.' She paused, searching for the right word. I was hideously aware of the pale pink blood vessels on her cheek. *'Pour l'esprit.'*

'Do you want your room cleaned, Jean? Jean?'

A 'no' drifted through the door. Or maybe he said 'go away'.

'I'm guessing it's pretty dank in there.'

'...need...'s...okay...'

'What?'

The door jerked open a fraction, a chain stretched across the gap. Behind it Jean-Yves stared out at me with half of his face, one eye scanning the hall. He was topless. A brewed scent wafted out from the room: a musty, salty combination.

'She still here?'

I tried to see in, but it was impossible. Grey-green light limped through the curtains, not illuminating anything, just sharpening the gloom.

'You should let her clean your room.'

'No.'

'When did you get that chain?'

His eye settled on me. I could smell his breath.

'It's always been there,' he spat, shutting the door with a puff of fetid air.

This wasn't true. I waited a moment.

'Jean! What am I supposed to do?' The door opened again maybe an inch. His right eye pressed into the space like a bloodshot sentinel.

'What do you mean?'

'Come on, you spend every day in this fucking room.'

The eye veered out into the hall, but I doubt he could see a thing.

'It's fine...'

'What's wrong?'

'Why are you playing dumb?' he whispered, as though afraid to speak the words aloud. I didn't know what he meant, wished I didn't, wished he wasn't thinking like this, that I could just – what?

'For god's sake,' I took a breath that seemed to envelope us both. 'What is it?'

'You've been talking to Mrs Su.'

'So what?'

'She's...'

'What?'

'The *Chinois*. You know.'

'Know what?'

'You *know*, Paul.'

'No, I *don't*.'

Jean sighed, 'I can't believe...' leaning his head against the door, his hair matted by sleep and flaked with dandruff. He looked up at me wearily through the crack. His eye jumped between mine as though trying to read something in them – 'What is it?' – then flicked to the hall again.

'Is she listening?'

'Just tell me.'

'I'm not...'

'*Please.*'

There was a long pause, a slow outlet of breath. 'You really want to know?'

I almost screamed, but managed to nod slowly.

'They want...' He looked back up at me, that single bloodshot eye, and swallowed, I could hear how dry his throat was. '...to eat us.'

Even after I'd made up my mind, I couldn't leave. I sat in my room, trying to read until the words were running off the page like hot ants. I considered writing more letters but saw only an endless stream of crumpled paper flying out the window, piles of dead letters in the street. I sat with my hand on the phone for a few minutes, then, after a devout spell of cursing the Monsieur for dragging us here, came back into the living room. The TV was on, but it was just noise, blending with the mutter of lunch-hour traffic like a secret message of goading, my hands taking on a life of their own, percussing table edges, window sills, thighs, my body feeling like a restless flight of moths. I told myself it was fear for my brother, of leaving him alone, but that wasn't it. I couldn't talk with anyone, couldn't read a sign. Finding this doctor was going to be impossible. I'd been lost before and this time felt the city would swallow me alive.

The Monsieur had once mentioned that when Mrs Su cleaned, nothing seemed to happen: no dust shifted, no magazines moved off the floor, but he'd find tapes of incense burning under the couch. Her instructions were similarly vague. I felt like I was being guided through time, as much as space: At Emperor's tea house, turn for Three-Ears-of-Corn Hall... Over the Bridge of Nine Turnings...

'How will I know it?'

'You see.'

'See what?'

'See sign.'

'A real sign? Of wood?'

She frowned up at me, eyes dark lines in the burnished skin of her face, but she said nothing else. If she'd been able to say more she would have, I told myself. I didn't believe it, but it got me out the door. I was even smiling as I came down on to the street; not because anything about this was funny – I was wishing I had my brother along, but knew that if he'd been well enough to come, I wouldn't have needed to go. It made me think of a book I'd read, how people say 'Catch 22' the way they say 'ironic'. They don't know what they mean.

Pale and lacking any dimensions, the sky was a soft white lid over the city. The rain had stopped. In its place were mounds of dirty paper, slumped like low hills of snow from a surrealist theatre piece. People were back on the street now, walking around the larger clumps, kicking through smaller ones, as if nothing strange had happened, as though a massive parade had passed down our street without my noticing, leaving it strewn with drifts of damp confetti, piled over cars, against store fronts, obscuring whole doorways. How had this happened? I stepped round a small mound to get a better look. Was my letter in there somewhere?

I felt myself straddling a fulcrum, teetering one way then the other. This is *exactly* why I didn't want to go looking for a 'doctor'. For a long second I didn't know which way I would fall. I thought of my brother in his room, eating only bread and pâté; Mrs Su crouched at the window; Shanghai, immense and blank to me, threaded by a few bright lonely routes. I leaned against a pillar and there, plastered wetly to the concrete, like an emissary from mystery, was Mrs Su's paper figure.

On Waibadu bridge nobody was going any faster or slower than anyone else. The sky was still fathomless, but it looked to rain again soon, the last downpour evaporating from the pavement beneath our feet, just to fall again in an hour or two. The air was stifling and wet and laced with the smell of bodies, sharp like lilies, but persistent like soup bones. Creamy brown water swirled past the caissons below. The Mansions' ancient brickwork seemed to leech into it, darkening the river in its shadow. Up ahead the verdigris cone of the Peace Hotel loomed, blotting out the early afternoon sun as I reached the bridge's end.

I'd heard we smell like old milk, to them.

I walked towards the Stock Exchange on Nanjing. It had opened the year before, in '86. It was the Monsieur's landmark, not mine, but I gravitated towards it. I could espouse some theory about it being a link to the world I knew, but what did I know? The stock market was strange to me, at least as alien as hanging charms in trees or sewing a dead man's pockets shut.

The crowd began to thicken around Sichuan Zhong until people were just standing, hardly moving. They didn't jostle, simply stood there. I was a head taller than anyone else, but got the impression people were deliberately not looking at me, restraining their curiosity. I heard drums and soon saw the red and green head, dinner-plate eyes of a dragon, its tasselled shell being foisted along the street. Fireworks cracked and hissed beneath red lanterns, the dancers' shoulders rising and falling. So this was the parade? I stooped to push towards the crowd's edge. Surely I would have heard this hullabaloo coming past?

I reached the curb and a green, huge-mouthed demon bent down as though to swallow my head. I ducked aside, across the road. Someone in white gloves shouted at me, but the audience was thinner and I pushed through to a side alley. Underfoot was strewn with trampled paper cups, newspaper and *la mien* plates.

Turning right on to Henan Lu, I slipped into the stream of people flowing south, down towards the Old Town. It was getting on to mid-afternoon and I remembered days like this in Catalonia, the shady drift of a crowd through the streets at Carnival, the loose exhaustion of moments after the spectacle. I walked past shop fronts and dingy, ad hoc-looking air-con units propped up by warped poles, street lights with inverted orange fruit-bowl shades, and the people, endless waves of people recycled through the scene for all I knew. Blank out the faces, the words, and it could have been anywhere.

Disparagingly or not, Shanghai was once called the 'Paris of the East'. It struck me as a confession of uncertainty, of the city's lack of distinction in the minds of its invaders. The Paris I knew clung to its throne grimly. It didn't have the distinction to spare – tourists brought it with them and then took it away, replenishing and reaping it daily.

Wearing their cameras like totems, clutches of *Chinois* tourists wandered slowly past the fruiterers, tailors, printmakers, artisans and hundred other merchants who bawled prices at them. Most of them kept to their huddles, descending en masse upon the occasional shop. They made me feel a little better. I turned right, then right again into an alley of closed grilles and unlit windows, the air tainted by something mechanical. There were a few pedestrians, a couple of salt-water sisters lingering in a doorway further up, an old *Chinois* smoking his pipe in a doorway. The smoke hung about him, undissipated. I came a little closer, stared for a long time at the sign above his head. Was it exactly the same? Like someone almost smiling.

A sign, she'd said.

Ha.

I walked up to the door and the old *Chinois* gazed up at me. His face reminded me of an old vaudeville mask. The happy one. But he wasn't smiling. He just gazed at me, eyes unfocused, the smoke rising around him and still not seeming to go anywhere.

'*Bonjour*,' I coughed. 'Is this the doctor's?'

He smiled and began to titter, gently, the laughter of birds.

'No Eng-eesh,' he mumbled, still staring vacantly as if I were hardly there.

He exhaled and fumes curled around me in ribbons so thick and vascular that I had to step out of them, through the doorway, still coughing. He did nothing to stop me, followed me with his eyes a few feet more, then returned to his vigil. The hallway was dim, leading up stairs to a door silvered with old, peeled paint. I stood there for a second, letting the moment settle on me. The symbols had been the same. How? I was trying to think, but no answer came. I realised I was clenching my teeth.

I knocked and the sepulchral sound vanished into the wood. There was a quiet echo, but I swear I heard it with my body, not my ears, an almost silent swelling of sound. Some of my tension lifted away and, without thinking, I knocked again. I was about to try it once more when I heard shuffling inside. The door opened.

'*Bonjour*,' I said, my tongue thick in my mouth. Large, widely spaced eyes were focused on me. 'Are you the doctor?'

He stood aside and ushered me into his small, warm, gloomy room, toward a pair of chairs. A little light fell from a window in the roof, giving on to a blank white sky. Behind us, from a row of cages, came the soft chirruping of crickets. Bamboo-print paper covered the walls. Nothing suggested a doctor's office, but according to Mrs Su, he wasn't one. Not exactly. He sat down opposite me.

'I am Lung…ah…?' The silence of his question hung for a moment before I saw what he was asking.

'Paul! Sorry.' I still felt dazed, as though the tension that left me a few seconds earlier had taken something else with it. I forced myself to sit erectly in the chair, to focus on him. In Tousec our skin tells our years, but I found it difficult with *Chinois*. His face was near bronze, dark yellow, almost grey around the cheeks. It could be he suffered from some disorder, a kidney disease. Perhaps he was sixty-five.

'I am not a doctor.' The skin at the corners of his mouth was pale and dry.

'I know. I'm not here for myself.'

'Of course...' He gave a dry croak, laughter, 'few people come to me on their own behalf.' Clean-shaven and bald, his head had a faintly triangular aspect to it. His voice was strange too, hissy, but his French...

'Your French is good.'

'Thank you. I've had long to master it.'

I wasn't sure what he meant, so I just smiled. He continued with his unblinking, reptilian stare. I suppose it was just his manner.

'I've come about my brother.'

'Please, tell me.'

I began to describe Jean's symptoms, but he shook his head. 'No. Earlier.'

So I told him about life with Jean-Yves, growing up with the boy who took half an hour to wash himself in the morning then made us late for school by touching every door along the way; who would vanish from class if told he could not use a pencil, only a pen; who picked every poppy seed from a biscuit he would only eat in the first place if it were perfect, crumbless. Lung sat motionless, listening to how my brother's catalogue of childhood foibles had eventually settled, but now returned, not the eccentricities of a nervous child exerting himself against the world, but the delusions of a damaged adult in retreat from it.

'He thinks that...'

Lung did not speak, but I almost heard him say, 'Yes?'

'...that people here...that they're...' I sighed far too loudly. 'He thinks they're trying to eat him.'

Hearing the words from my own mouth it seemed so ridiculous I had a sudden urge to laugh. But somewhere was the fixed and certain knowledge that it wasn't funny; that if tragedy and comedy were the same thing, they were neither. My chest tightened and for a moment I saw my fear as a ship, massive, moored to a wharf in a hurricane...battering, demolishing it. My brother! There was a fizzing sensation across my cheeks and I realised I was about to cry.

'Sorry.'

'Never mind,' he rasped. 'He is aggressive?'

'What?'

'Is your brother an aggressive?' I shook my head, wiped my face. Paranoid, yes, and deranged, but not violent.

'Good,' said Lung, and the word took a moment to percolate through the gauze of my efforts to resist further tears. 'I cannot treat violence. It is outside my...*ch'i*.' He gave an almost lipless smile, his teeth barely visible, then looked down at his hands, as though making a calculation. 'He suffers an excess of the *yin*...'

I must have looked sceptical, because he raised a long, sharp-nailed finger.

'Please, do not be alarmed.'

I was clenching my hands uselessly in my lap.

'This is way of speaking...a form of the information ...Another way to say would be...that his immune is low...lowered?' I nodded. 'I have seen this...' a hacking noise, it might have been a cough '…after opium wars when…your people were…here.'

He couldn't have meant that literally, but the ponderous, almost classical care of his French helped me to pull myself together, to think of Jean-Yves as a distant subject; less a person than an abstract problem.

Lung went on and the vagueness I'd felt changed shape as I tried to follow him. Exactly how he got so much from so little I was never sure, but I remembered a doctor's surgery I once visited, where I was diagnosed before I'd even sat down. I was nine and for a long time afterward believed that doctors worked by an elaborate and largely infallible magic.

My brother had been going to school near Toulouse, a region in which Catholicism informed the habits of its people, but could hardly be said to condition their lives. A few parallel superstitions were still observed: one poured milk with the left hand, and the first *miel* of the spring was thrown in the river at first flood, but this was the limit. Incantations gave way to a sort of deferred comprehension, as fear once reserved for the devil's blight dissolved in a vague understanding of pesticides. In this reduced psychic climate, my brother had his work cut out for him, being what Lung described as 'a sensitive' – his overactive mind, lost to the older powers, had latched on to smaller concerns: pencils and soap, doors, crumbs…

'This is not uncommon in your part of the world, these, ah…you say "nervous" disorders?'

I nodded.

'They will be very more common in next decade.' He paused for a long moment, as though pondering his grammar.

'Whichever way you like...the mind, body, one extend from other. There is no...division to be making. When body fights disease, it tires. When mind fights...life, it fatigues.'

'*Life*?'

'No, sorry, there is no word. Your brother is very open. He notices very much, no?'

I let my head fall forwards; the thought of it, of his opposition to life itself, left me feeling clogged and impotent. How did you fight something like that?

'Here, in Shanghai, China, the spirits still alive...ghosts walk with us, gods watch...'

'But I don't believe –'

'It does not matter what you believe. Faith of people plagues your brother...Whether these things exist or no...this is not a point...your brother, Jan –'

'Jean-Yves.'

'He is reaction to small...indications, you would say, everywhere, of spirits, ancestors, dragons,' he coughed, '...Yu Huang.'

'So he has to leave? I don't –'

'No, no, he is too far now.' His tongue moved in short, excited arcs across his lips. 'He is weak, needs...boost.'

He reminded me briefly of Jane Fonda, as though a few stretches were all my brother needed. His mind had latched on to these minute details, immersed in an atmosphere you couldn't see, only detect – spirits or inflections of something more mechanical, the city invisible, China itself, her history, I couldn't say, but the uncertainty – all these uncertainties – made me jittery, like my concern was a physical thing and as I let it go, piece by piece, I lost the steadying elements of myself. It was a ridiculous idea. What was wrong with me? I felt nauseated.

Lung watched my fingers tapping an anti-rhythm on the chair arm. Unblinking, unmoving, he seemed embedded in the room, as much a fact of it as the furniture, until he smiled, bared teeth worn to sharp yellow points.

The door beside the fish tank opened on darkness. From a jar on the shelf beside it Lung removed a torch. He flicked the switch, banged it on his palm and a dusky light came on. He looked at me, gave a phlegmy snicker.

'Magic.'

Coarse wooden stairs spiralled down into darkness, the torch weak and illuminating a few steps ahead. In the reflected light Lung's head was a knobbly, fishy grey. It was all I could see of him.

'Your brother, he is acute,' he explained as we curled downwards. The walls were plaster, stained by water and age, cracked with dry bubbles of decay. 'Some I treat without going to this...level...but for him we must fetch the ingredient.' He hopped a broken step.

'What?' I asked, nearly falling over something narrow and spongy. He exhaled as though he had stubbed a toe, didn't hear me. I was still turning over what Lung had said about my brother, about China, his resistance to things we couldn't see.

'Why cannibalism?'

Lung stopped and swung the torch in my face.

'When afraid of the present, people retreat into ways from past...old knowledges.' He made a clicking sound at the back of his throat. 'Your brother goes too far.'

Time was hard to gauge. Stairs changed to stone; plaster turned to earth. My ears popped and the air became damp and cold, laden with its own sluggish weight as we straightened out into a rock-cut hallway. It smelled of something, but I couldn't name it.

Ahead the blackness widened and Lung crept out of sight. There was a tired metallic grating sound and a tremor, like a vibration too fast or high pitched to hear. Soft patches of light began to spread across the roof, closing out islands of darkness.

With no better response, I recoiled. I felt Lung's cold firm hand support me. Walls I had assumed were a few metres away were more like sixty or eighty. The roof was not a ceiling, but a vault with acres of stalactites. Across the floor a thousand stalagmites ranged in their weird geologic conference.

'It is surprising, I am sure.'

'Are those…what is that light?'

'Insects. You can hear, no?' He closed his eyes and hummed a long, wiry note. Out over the flow of rock it was quiet, but not silent – somewhere water was dripping and, behind it, everywhere, was the edge of a sound, its leftovers, like something from the confused edge of sleep. Maybe that's what he meant.

Lung walked down a short flight of hewn stairs and began to make his way through a corridor of stalagmites. He was still humming as he disappeared amongst them, a zoetrope figure in and out of the frozen rock spires, some smaller, most taller than he was. I tottered down after him, letting my hands linger on their coolness as I passed by. I could scarcely believe it, felt like I was losing the battle, but my mind was taking the tactile approach, as though if I could touch enough of these things… When I caught up, Lung was approaching a shelf of assorted objects. There were other shelves, an arc of them tucked out of sight with the air of a surreptitious museum, a raider's cache.

'How far down are we?' I asked, knowing it wasn't the right question.

Smiling like a knife, Lung said, 'One would have difficult to dig here,' then turned to the shelf and began to rustle among the faded objects, all of them the same stale yellow. For a moment, this was all I could see, their familiar curves and notchings, the holes and functional edges. Then I saw what I was looking at.

'Whose bones?'

And I think it was this moment, this indivisible instant, that I ran out of awe. I wasn't sure whether it was just that afternoon or recent months, or something that had been creeping steadily toward me for longer than I even knew, but a kind of calmness descended. Though it wasn't calmness, not quite.

'This is what we need. Yes,' he mumbled, descending into raspy Chinese. He turned around and held up a bone. In the full glare of the glazed cave light it shone a sickly green, small and bent like a bracket. The not-calm had expanded within me. I couldn't think how these bones might have managed to be here – I wasn't convinced of any of this – but at that second it didn't seem to matter.

'Great. What bone is that?'

'You don't needing to understand...' distracted, his French was suffering '...for it to work.' I was thinking about that when something clunked and the air seemed to go abruptly still. Lung spat a phrase, a harsh string of consonants, and the light began to fade. He grabbed my arm, dragged me back towards the doorway. I stumbled along, his nails digging painfully into my skin.

'I think...' he tossed the words over his shoulder, 'we

take ourselves away...' and we were almost halfway to the hall '...before darkness...' when something small and hard bounced off my arm '...find us.' There was a rasping sound, close to Lung's own laugh but far louder, as of ice-shelfs cracking apart. We ran toward the outline of the hallway, black against the falling night.

The dark trek back up the stairs filled my legs with cold oil. When we finally reached his room I sat in the chair, staring at Lung in his stillness, recessed once more into the furnishings. I couldn't summon the energy to ask what happened. After several minutes of exhausted silence he stood up and went to one of the cages. He thrust a hand inside. A frantic chirping passed from cage to cage, filling the small room, then died away as he lifted the struggling insect out. He took it to the table and laid it there. I expected it to fly away, but it just lay there.

He pulled a jar from the shelf beside him. It was filled with a thick dark liquid like molasses that he poured into a smaller jar. He crushed the bone with a pestle, wiped the dust into the small jar, and looked back at me.

'I am almost done, excuse please me.'

He turned away, picked up the cricket and, as though whispering to it, brought it to his mouth. There was a small noise, like the breaking of a tiny bone, an ear bone, then he made a few more movements. When he came back to his seat, he handed me the jar.

'What's this?'

'I would say... *yin*.' He blinked carefully. 'You would say... anti-psychotic,' like he was reading from a textbook, 'blocking D and HT receptors... to be preventing schizo-typal behaviours.'

'I wouldn't say that,' I smiled, and Lung made a slow rasping sound, another laugh. He held the jar out to me.

'Take it.' Then, as though anticipating a question I hadn't yet thought to ask, he said, 'There is no cost.'

'But I –'

He spread his wide hands, their sharp nails – a refusal. 'Your brother…Jean?'

'Jean-Yves.'

'He needs to drink it.'

'Okay.'

'At least half. All is better.'

'Right,' I said, standing up. We were face to face. I could see the texture of his skin, almost like scales, and I wondered again whether he was all right. His throat looked red, flushed. He wasn't watching me so much as resting his eyes on my face. It was discomforting. I looked around the room again, at the cages, the wallpaper, the endless forest of bamboo that circled the walls. Then I looked more closely. It was astonishing. The pattern was *hand-painted*, as though seen through the finest mist imaginable. I looked back at him, then at the wall, speechless.

'You painted all this?'

'As with French, I have had the time.'

Even standing, he was utterly still, as though bled of the motion that most of us never live long enough to lose. I really had no idea how old he was, what sort of doctor he was or wasn't, let alone whether I should trust this potion of his, but it was time to go. Holding up the jar, I said, 'Thanks very much. I don't know if –'

'You will try it,' he said, making it hard to tell if this was an order or a prediction.

★

The smoking *Chinois* had gone, but one of the girls was still lingering further up the alley. Her head turned as I stepped into the alley, then flicked back to waiting. Somewhere in the west the sun was crossing the space between clouds and horizon, swathing the sky in yellow that dipped to a wild orange in its troughs.

When I reached the river it was glazed in a fiery light that only made the water look blacker. I stared at it a long time, resting the jar on the roadside wall. My mind felt washed out, burnt down. I knew there was something I'd missed about today, maybe a single detail that could have brought the whole thing into focus: Jean-Yves, Lung, this jar of goo, but I'd missed it. Or maybe there was no detail, no focus. I had no energy left to wonder with. Someone passed behind me and I turned around: his face creased, a slight crimp to his mouth and a tightening of his jaw as he saw me. He walked quickly past, the stiffened gait of someone being watched.

The jar was clay, its glaze slick in my hand. I pulled the wooden lid off and looked at the linctus inside: black like the water below, but more viscous. It smelled of nothing, just an old jar, yet charged with something else – bone and crickets? What did I know about Lung. Maybe it was stupid, even dangerous to think of feeding this to my brother. There was no way to tell. As though the universe had briefly and imperfectly parted in two, I saw myself heave it into the Huangpu, a slow black stream of rheum tracing an arc behind it...

I put the lid back, started walking up the river. Night was rising blue in the east and the Bund was still thick with traffic, but I don't remember hearing it. I walked beneath a bare row of plum blossoms, reflected faintly in the river.

Someone had tied red charm strings to their trunks and a few still hung there, but most had fallen off, lying scuffed and broken on the pavement. I walked on and it was a few minutes before I thought to wonder about them.

If they fell off, did they still work?

AUTHOR PROFILES

Henry Feltham was born in 1979, in a hospital that is now an apartment block. His first twenty years featured loud noises, mayonnaise and the persistent smell of chlorine, but were otherwise a blur. In this new century he is exploring rural New Zealand. He spends the mornings writing and the afternoons devising a series of feeble distractions. Much to his surprise, he is married.

Briar Grace-Smith is an award-winning writer of plays, scripts and short stories. Her first major play, *Nga Pou Wahine*, earned her the 1995 Bruce Mason Playwriting Award, and *Purapurawhetu* won Best New Zealand Play at the 1997 Chapman Tripp Theatre Awards. In 2000 Grace-Smith received the Arts Foundation Laureate Award and *Haruru Mai* premiered at the International Festival of the Arts. Her first television play, *In a Fish Skin Suit*, premiered on TV3. In 2002 Grace-Smith was a finalist for the Prize in Modern Letters. Her work has been performed at festivals and conferences in Ireland and Sydney; her play *Purapurawhetu* toured Canada and Greece. In 2003 Grace-Smith was the Writer in Residence at Victoria University, and in 2006, *100 Cousins* premiered in Auckland. She lives with her husband and children in Paekakariki, on the Kapiti Coast. Grace-Smith is affiliated to Nga Puhi and Ngati Wai iwi in the far north.

Kingi McKinnon was born in Auckland and at the age of seven moved back to the Waikato. Severe illness forced McKinnon to leave school at fifteen, after which he worked on his father's farm. Since then he has held many jobs, including truck driving, construction work and coal mining. While in plaster and recovering from an ankle injury, McKinnon began to write for children. He is a part-time tutor in creative writing at Waiariki Polytechnic. He has contributed to several anthologies and is published in Australia, England and Germany. McKinnon has written four novels, *The Friday Frights, Whitebait Fritters, When the Kehua Calls* and *Tales from the Swamp*. In 1996 *Whitebait Fritters* was short-listed for the AIM Children's Book Award and in 2003 *When the Kehua Calls* was short-listed for the New Zealand Post Children's Book Award.

Philippa Swan is a Wellington landscape architect and magazine columnist. 'Life Coach' is her first piece of published fiction. Swan studied geography at Otago University before gaining a degree in landscape architecture from the University of Melbourne. She has worked in local government and as a design tutor, and established her own landscape architecture practice. Swan began writing for magazines in 1995 and is a regular contributor to *New Zealand Gardener*. In 2001, her book *Life (and Death) in a Small City Garden* was published by Godwit. Swan has recently moved to the suburbs and is raising two children. Her link with the outside world is maintained by her columns for *New Zealand Gardener* and *Cuisine*. On fine days she likes to work in her garden. She enjoys growing gourmet vegetables and cooking, but what she enjoys most is writing.

Brian Turner has been publishing poems since the 1960s. He has published best-selling sports biographies (with Colin Meads, Josh Kronfeld, Anton Oliver and his brother Glenn Turner), and his other books include the autobiographical *Somebodies and Nobodies: Growing up in an Extraordinary Sporting Family*, *Timeless Land* (with Grahame Sydney and Owen Marshall) and numerous collections of poetry, the most recent being *Footfall*, which was short-listed for the 2006 Montana New Zealand Book Awards. Turner won the 1978 Commonwealth Poetry Prize and the 1993 New Zealand Book Award for Poetry. In 1984 he was the Robert Burns Fellow at the University of Otago and in 1997 he was Writer in Residence at the University of Canterbury. From 2003 to 2005, Turner was the Te Mata Estate Poet Laureate. Turner was born in Dunedin in 1944 and now lives in Oturehua, Central Otago.

Phoebe Wright was born in Christchurch in 1990. She started writing for a class assignment in Year 10 and found herself unable to stop. She has enjoyed some success while at Burnside High School, winning the Peter Smart Writing Competition and having short stories published in the *Re-draft* series for young writers. Inspiration for her writing comes from a fascination and love for the absurdity of the human condition, and from a memorable four months travelling around Europe in a cramped campervan. Her other interests include reading, painting and cacti, and she has shared her life with several generations of pet rats.

Representing booksellers and publishers

Proudly sponsored by:

NEW ZEALAND BOOK COUNCIL
Te Kaunihera Pukapuka o Aotearoa

ARTS COUNCIL OF NEW ZEALAND *TOI AOTEAROA*

 HarperCollins*Publishers*

COMMUNITY POLYTECHNIC
Te Kura Matatini o Whitireia